USING THE
INTERNET
IN SECONDARY
SCHOOLS

TES
THE TIMES EDUCATIONAL SUPPLEMENT

USING THE
INTERNET
IN SECONDARY SCHOOLS

2ND EDITION

ETA DE CICCO, MIKE FARMER
& JAMES HARGRAVE

Routledge
Taylor & Francis Group

LONDON AND NEW YORK

This edition published 2013 by routledge
2 Park Square, Milton Park, Abingdon, Oxon OX14 4RN
711 Third Avenue, New York, NY 10017

Routledge is an imprint of the Taylor & Francis Group, an informa business

First published in 1998
Second edition 2001

The views expressed in this book are those of the authors and are not necessarily the same as those of *The Times Educational Supplement*.

British Library Cataloguing in Publication Data

A CIP record for this book is available from the British Library.

ISBN 0 7494 3459 7

Typeset by Jean Cussons Typesetting, Diss, Norfolk

Contents

Contents

Foreword

The Internet is having a fundamental effect in many fields from big business to communications and, of course, education. As it becomes ever more widely available, so its influence will continue to grow. As this happens, the need to teach children about and using the Internet will also become more important.

Now that just about every secondary school in the United Kingdom has a connection to the Internet, the fun should really begin to start. As schools get more and more computers with access to the World Wide Web, an ever-increasing number of pupils will be able to search Web sites for information, use e-mail regularly, take part in online discussions, chats and videoconferences, and create their own sites. Likewise, teachers will be able to make use of the vast range of online resources available in their teaching.

The Internet has started to change education, and the pace of that change will continue to speed up. All of this does not spell the end of other ways of working or learning. Nor is the technological revolution going to be without problems, even when schools amass sufficient hardware and appropriate software.

Recent OECD research has concluded that students do not regard the Internet as a replacement for books. Furthermore, they often have trouble finding the information they need online, and have even more difficulty deciding whether the information they do find is reliable or not. Teachers must not make the mistake of thinking that students know it all when it comes to the Internet, even if they seem to be relatively comfortable with using parts of it. Many students want guidance, and all students need to develop and improve their online skills.

This book will show you how to help them do so and how to make the best possible use of online resources in the classroom. The Internet is an incredible phenomenon that potentially will have a greater effect on the world – and on education – than television. It has so much to offer but need not be overwhelming with this as your guide.

Bob Doe
Editor, The Times Educational Supplement

Preface

Education is the government's number one priority for the millennium. Initiatives, such as the National Grid for Learning (NGfL) and the University for Industry (UfI), have been set up to create a framework of opportunities in which individuals of all ages can learn. It is the intention of government that all schools will be connected to the 'superhighway' by the year 2002 and that all children will leave full-time education Information Technology-literate.

The British government launched the initial framework of a National Grid for Learning (NGfL) in November 1998. Now, the NGfL is the national focal point for learning on the Internet in the United Kingdom. Since its launch, it has grown from a few hundred pages to well over two thousand pages of indexed content. Its structure can accommodate the needs of learners in all sectors of education and of all age groups.

One benefit of accessing content on the Grid is that you can be sure that all contributors have been through an approval process that includes agreeing to the NGfL's Ground Rules and Code of Conduct. In conjunction with its partner site, The Virtual Teacher Centre, it provides the national focus for raising educational standards, particularly in numeracy and literacy.

With the introduction of the National Grid for Learning, it becomes even more important for all teachers to be confident and competent in using ICT (Information and Communications Technology) effectively in their teaching. Although the training of all student teachers now includes an element of ICT, practising teachers still require help in discovering ways in which to use ICT appropriately and successfully in the classroom.

As a consequence, the New Opportunities Fund (NOF) (http://www.nof.org.uk/) under Lottery funding has been set up to allow certain approved training providers to provide practising teachers with training in ICT. All NOF training must meet the requirements set out in the specification provided by NOF.

The specifications try to ensure that teachers develop the knowledge and skills necessary to access and exploit the electronic information and sources that will support their professional development. Above all, teachers must be provided with the opportunities to apply the knowledge, understanding and skills they gain via the NOF training to their classroom activities.

The main objective of the NOF training is on teachers developing the ability to use ICT effectively to achieve subject-related goals, and this book is specifically aimed at supporting this objective.

The book provides staff with lesson plans, based on material downloaded from the Internet, particularly the World Wide Web (Web), and covers Key Stages 3 to 4. All lesson plans reference the source Web sites and address specific National Curriculum subjects at the two Key Stage levels. In addition, the book provides technical details about the Internet tools and services mentioned within the lesson plans.

Part 1

Using the Internet in Schools

1

Basic tips on using the Net

These next three chapters are designed to encourage you to use the Internet in a more productive manner. Although you may have surfed the Web already, there's much more to learn about the Web and other Internet (Net) tools. This isn't as hard as it might sound – and in fact it will probably be a lot of fun!

We will look at how to make best use of a Web browser, give some general tips for using the Web and then look at some more advanced topics such as downloading and plug-ins.

Browsing the Web

Types of browsers

For PC and Macintosh users there are two main Web browsers, Netscape Navigator and Microsoft Internet Explorer. Internet 'addicts' can argue for hours about which one is 'the best' but in fact they are both very similar and do exactly the same thing although in slightly different ways.

By mid-2000, Netscape had reached version 4.75 and Internet Explorer version 5.5. However, some people are still using older versions and although these work just as well, they might not handle the newer Web features. Generally most features work with version 4.0 and later of Netscape and Internet Explorer.

PC and Macintosh users who don't like the browser that they have on their machine can download another type from the Internet. In fact, you can often run more than one browser on your machine. Latest versions and more information about browsers can be found at:

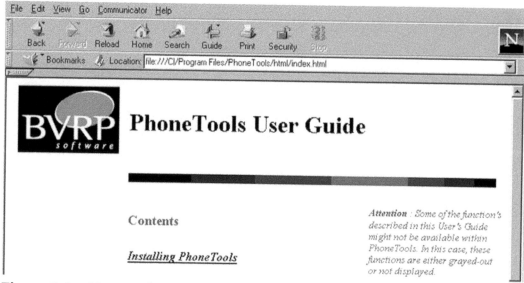

Figure 1.1 *Netscape browser*

Netscape:
http://www.netscape.com

Internet Explorer:
http://www.microsoft.com/ie

Take me home!

It is quite common to lose your way whilst surfing the Web. There are so many links to follow and places to go. If this happens, click 'Home' in your browser and you will be taken back to your selected 'Home' Page. This is either the Web site of your Internet Service Provider or another page you have selected for yourself. Often in a school or company this will be the Home Page of the organization owning the computer.

TIP

You can change the page that you go to when the 'Home' button is clicked.

In Internet Explorer, first open the page you want as your Home Page in the browser. Select *Tools* in the toolbar, choose *Internet Options* and then click on the *Use Current* button in the 'Home Page' area.

In Netscape, select *Edit* in the toolbar, choose *Preferences* and then the *Navigator* section. In the Home Page box, insert the address or URL of the page you'd like to allocate as your Home. These instructions may vary depending on the type and version of the browser that you will be using.

> **TIP**
>
> Sometimes people refer to a Web page address (for example http://www.bbc.co.uk) as a URL. This stands for Universal Resource Locator.

Searching for information

You will need to know how to search for information and this is where search tools come in handy. Chapter 3 of this book contains all you need to know about using search tools and getting the information you want from the Web.

Take me straight there (URLs)

If you already have the URL (address or Universal Resource Locator) of the Web site you want to go to, just place the cursor over the 'Address' window (in Explorer this is labelled *Address* while in Netscape it is called *Location*), highlight the address that might already be there, replace it with your URL and press return/enter.

> **TIP**
>
> To save time, with most browsers (including Netscape and Internet Explorer) you can key in a Web site address without the '**http://**' prefix, for example:
>
> http://www.becta.org.uk
>
> can be keyed in as:
>
> www.becta.org.uk

Help! It doesn't work! Error messages and URLs

When you click on a link or type in an address, you may get an error message rather than the site that you want. Before giving up, take a look at the tips below.

> **TIP**
>
> When typing in a Web address make sure to copy it accurately, in particular remembering to type lower case and upper case letters as they are written. For example:
>
> http://www.uce.ac.uk/faculties/educhome.htm

will work but if you typed in:

http://www.uce.ac.uk/faculties/EDUCHOME.htm

it wouldn't work and nor would:

http://www.uce.ac.uk/faculties/Educhome.htm

TIP

The most common error message is '404 File Not Found' or 'the file cannot be found'.

If you type in a Web address or follow a link and you get this error message or find it doesn't work, try removing the end part of the address, from right to left, until you get to a page that works.

For example, if you type in:

http://www.bbc.co.uk/history/programmes/hob/dynasty.html

but get an error message '404 File Not Found', first of all try:

http://www.bbc.co.uk/history/programmes/hob/

thus removing the end of the address. See if this works, if not then try:

http://www.bbc.co.uk/history/programmes/

thus removing the next end part. Continue to remove all the parts on the right-hand side until you find something that works. This is often successful because Web site administrators move the location of files on a Web site but the links pointing to them are not always changed.

If you still can't get the link to work, the site has either changed address completely or is no longer available.

Slow loading pages

If you go to a Web site and it doesn't work or appears very slow to download, first try clicking the *Stop* button on your Web browser and then select *Re-load* or *Refresh*. If you still find it impossible, or slow to view, there might be a problem at that site or on the Internet. Try it again later in the day.

What's in an address? Top-level domains

You may wonder what Internet addresses mean and how they work. The address www.bbc.co.uk should provide a clue. Look at the address from the right-hand side and read to the left. The part of the address at the right-hand end is called the *top-level domain*. This is usually a country code or alternatively something like .com, .edu or in this case, .uk.

For historical reasons sites in America don't usually have a country code so a site ending in .edu is usually in America. Table 1.1 explains some of the more common top-level domains.

Table 1.1 *Top-level domains*

Domain	Description
The following top-level domains have been with us for years:	
.com	Company
.org	Non-profit organization
.edu	Educational organization
.net	Network resource
.gov	Government organization
.mil	Military organization
.ca	Canada
.uk	United Kingdom
.fr	France
.jp	Japan
.au	Australia
.de	Germany
.nl	Netherlands
A number of other top-level domains are being suggested as additions to the above. These are:	
.firm	Businesses and firms
.shop	Businesses offering goods to purchase
.web	Organizations with activities related to the Web
.arts	Organizations emphasizing cultural and entertainment activities
.rec	Organizations offering recreation and entertainment activities.
.info	Organizations providing information services
.nom	Organizations that want a personal nomenclature (*nom de plume*)

Within some of these top-level domains, you get what is known as *sub-domains*. For example, sites ending in .uk also have something in front of this to indicate what sort of UK site it is, such as .co.uk, which denotes a UK company. Table 1.2 explains the more common UK sub-domains.

Sometimes, using this information, you can even guess the address of an organization's Web page. For example, the BBC's site is:

http://www.bbc.co.uk

The *www* part of the address is often considered a Web site address and is more a convention than anything else.

Table 1.2   *Sub-domain levels*

Sub-domain	Description
.co.uk	UK company
.org.uk	UK non-profit organization
.gov.uk	UK government
.ac.uk	UK academic organization
.sch.uk	UK School
.mil.uk	UK military organization
.pol.uk	UK police
.net.uk	UK network resource

Remember that site – *Bookmarks* and *Favorites*

If you go to a Web site that you think you will want to refer to again, you can add it to a list which will facilitate easy access in the future. Netscape uses the term *Bookmarks* and Internet Explorer uses *Favorites* to represent this list but they are both really the same thing.

In your browser, access the page that you want to add and then choose the *Bookmarks* or *Favorites* menu. Click on the *Add to* option. The page's address has now been added to your list of *Bookmarks/Favorites*.

If you want to return to that site in the future, just click on the *Bookmarks* or *Favorites* menu and you will see the name of the site listed. Select it with the mouse and your browser will take you there without you having to type in its address.

TIP

You can organize your *Bookmarks* or *Favorites* into neat lists under headings, therefore grouping similar sites together, for example *children's sites* or *sport*. This makes sense when you have a lot of sites in your list.

To edit your list in Internet Explorer, choose *Favorites* and then *Organize Favorites*. In Netscape select the *Bookmarks* menu and then *Edit Bookmarks*.

These instructions may vary depending on the type and version of the browser that you will be using.

Downloading files from the Internet

After surfing the Web, there comes a time to move on to some more advanced uses of the Net. In addition to viewing information and pictures on the Net, you can also download them and other files to your computer. Some of the exercises in the curriculum section of the book will require you to download files, including sound, video and programs, and sometimes install and run those programs.

Before starting: anti-virus software

Before you download anything to your computer you need to check a few things out. First, make sure that your computer has some sort of *anti-virus* software installed that will protect against downloading files containing viruses. It is not unusual to get a virus with a file downloaded from the Internet, so take every precaution. If you do not have anti-virus software you can buy it from a computer supplier or obtain a demo or trial version on a cover disk from a computer magazine or download one from the Internet.

Make sure that the site from which you are downloading looks reputable and is not offering anything that sounds too good to be true. You should be safe downloading from the sites of well-known companies but avoid sites that offer commercial software *free of charge*. Such software might be illegal and the price you pay could be a virus on your computer.

Shareware, freeware, licences

Before downloading programs that you intend to use, check to see if they are free or if you will be required to pay a fee after a period of use.

Many programs available on the Internet are *shareware*. These programs can be freely distributed and tried out on your computer (usually for up to 30 days) but you will need to pay a small fee if you want to *register* the program and continue to use it. Some programs will stop working if you don't pay this fee. Shareware programs should come with information about how you can pay the fee and register.

Several other programs, such as many Web browsers and plug-ins, are made available free to users and no fee is involved. These programs are known as *freeware*.

Finding the right file

If you want to download a particular piece of software or file, then you can search for it. See Chapter 3 for more information and tips on searching.

Some sites offer the choice of many versions of the same software to download. Make sure the file you choose is appropriate for your computer. For example, if you have a Macintosh, don't choose to download a program that will only run under Windows 98 or Windows 2000.

Some files will only work if you have certain hardware and/or software on your computer. For example, to play a sound file you will need a sound card and speakers connected to your computer. In addition, you may need the correct software for the type of sound you are downloading. The site from which you are obtaining the file should make this clear.

Sometimes you will have to click on boxes and fill in forms before you can download files. You may need to give your name and e-mail address. This is generally safe, and in some cases you have no choice if you want to download their software.

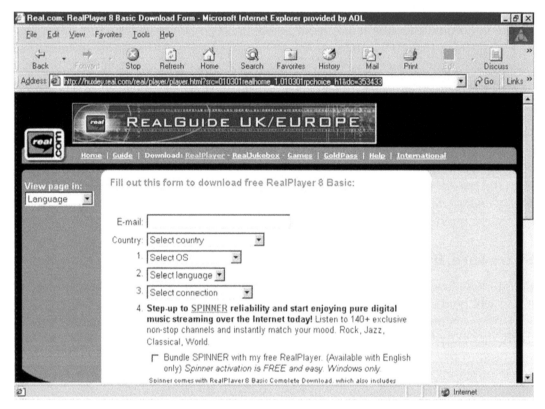

Figure 1.2 *Downloading files*

You may find that certain sites give you an option to download from several other Web servers in different parts of the world as well as from their own site. These sites are known as *mirror* sites as they contain a mirror image of the files on the main site.

If given the option, always choose a site as near to your country as you can when downloading files. For example, if there is a site in London and you are in the UK then choose that site, as it will probably speed up your download time.

Where to place files

Once you have located the right file to download, you will need to click on a link to begin the download to your computer. PC and Macintosh users will be prompted with a box asking where you want to save the file and what you want to call it.

The important thing is to remember where you save the file on your computer. Many people create a special directory/folder called *downloads* or something similar to keep track of downloaded files.

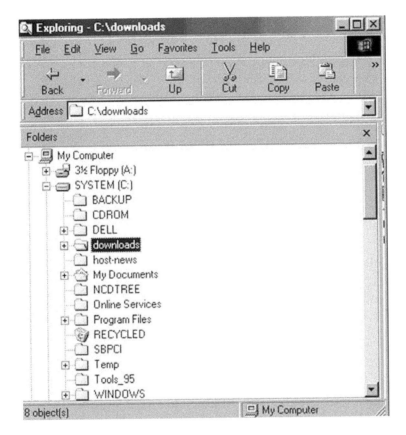

Figure 1.3 *A downloads folder on a PC*

If the computer suggests a name for the file then accept this, otherwise make one up that is meaningful to you. In any case remember and *write down* the name of the file and the directory/folder that you are saving it in.

Sometimes, you may be given the option to open the program straight away rather than save the file to use later. This is a good option if you want to use the program online and not save it for future use.

Patience, and problems!

Downloading files can be time-consuming but thankfully most Web browsers give you some indication of the progress of the download and how much longer it should take to complete the task.

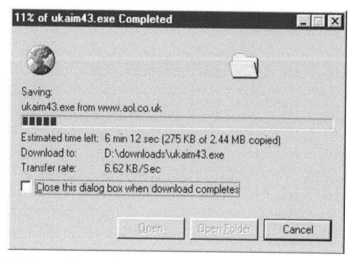

Figure 1.4   *Dialogue box indicating progress of the download*

Often downloads progress smoothly without any problems but sometimes you may have some difficulties. If you lose your connection to the Internet in the middle of a download then sadly you will have to start again from scratch. This is even the case if 99 per cent of the file has been downloaded.

Occasionally a download will seem to just stop working altogether or become painfully slow. If this happens, click on *Stop* in your browser and try the download again.

If you still have the same problem then try again sometime later as the site is probably busy dealing with a large number of users. In fact, some sites limit the number of people that can download at any one time, in which case you will get a message asking you to try again later.

Installing downloaded files

Once your file is successfully downloaded you may get a message telling you that the download is complete or the download progress box may just disappear. If you are using a modem it is best to close your connection to the Internet at this point and to close your Web browser and any programs that may be running.

You now need to locate the program that you have downloaded. Of course, you wrote down the name of the file and the directory as suggested earlier.

Newer versions of Internet Explorer give the option to 'open' a file that has just been downloaded, which is a useful feature if you tend to forget the names of downloaded files!

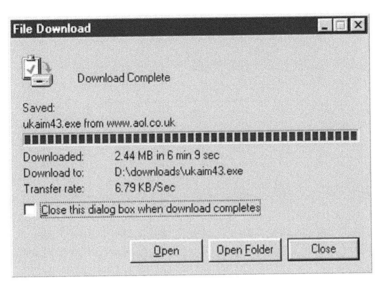

Figure 1.5 *Options after downloading a file*

It may be that the file you have downloaded is compressed in some way and you will need to uncompress it before you can install it. See Chapter 3 for more details on the different types of compression and tools to deal with them.

When you have located the program, double-click on it to begin the installation process. What happens now will depend on the software that you are installing. Usually, some kind of install program will appear and guide you through the installation process.

If not, you may get a black screen and a message about uncompressing files. If this happens on a PC, then you can look again in the directory in which you placed the program for another file called *setup* and double-click on this to complete the installation process. Macintosh users will probably need to uncompress the file first (Chapter 3, Other Internet tools of the trade). In some cases, you will need to restart your computer before you can use the program that you have installed.

Plug-ins, sound and video

Web browsers are capable of doing more than just displaying text and graphics. You can also display animated graphics, sound and video. However, to do this, you may

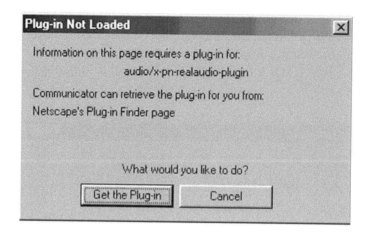

Figure 1.6   *Site request for a plug-in*

need to download a special program that works with your Web browser. These are often referred to as *plug-ins*.

Often a site will tell you that, to view their video or listen to their audio files, you need a particular plug-in and will give a pointer to a location where you can download that plug-in.

To install a plug-in, just follow the instructions on downloading (see Downloading files from the Internet, above). Plug-ins may be required to complete some of the activities in the curriculum section of this book.

The latest versions of some Web browsers have the most popular plug-ins already installed (see Chapter 3 for more details).

Online safety and unsuitable material

Most sites on the Internet are perfectly decent and suitable for people of all ages. However, there are some sites that are certainly unsuitable for pupils and young children as they contain pornography or other unsuitable material. There may also be child protection issues around the use of chat rooms and UseNet groups (see Chapter 4, Talk! Talk! Talk!).

Some Internet Service Providers offer a special *filtered* service to block access to many of these sites. Some even offer a filtered service with regard to certain 'unsuitable' newsgroups (see Chapter 4, Talk! Talk! Talk!). Alternatively, you can obtain special software that blocks sites on your machine, such as *Surf Watch* or *Cyber Sitter.*

Whilst these tools are certainly useful and worth investigating, none of them are totally successful and some have the side effect of blocking perfectly decent sites and useful activities.

The most effective way to ensure that pupils do not access unsuitable material is to plan adequate adult supervision and to educate pupils about the subject. Make sure that Internet-linked computers are in public places where pupils can be easily seen and supervised.

Many schools require pupils and sometimes parents to sign an agreement before they access the Internet, where they promise to adhere to rules regarding the viewing and downloading of offensive materials. As part of the agreement, if a pupil breaks the rules, Internet access can be suspended for a period of time or indefinitely. Example agreements and letters for parents can be found at:

http://safety.ngfl.gov.uk/

Becta produce a series of information sheets about different topics of interest to teachers. Here, you can find information on such matters as copyright and safety on the Internet:

http://www.becta.org.uk/technology/infosheets/index.html

Resources

Software sources

Windows and Macintosh Internet Software Site:

http://tucows.rmplc.co.uk

General Software — including anti-virus, shareware, and filtering software:

http://www.shareware.com
http://www.download.com

Browsers resource site:

http://www.browsers.com

Note that as browsers can take up to an hour to download it may be easier to load a new browser from the free front-cover CD ROMs on many PC magazines. *PC Pro* and *Personal Computer World* usually have the latest versions.

Online safety and filtering products

http://safety.ngfl.gov.uk/
http://www.becta.org.uk/technology/infosheets/index.html

2

Using the Web in schools

Connecting to the Internet

Each school is different, so giving advice on how to connect to the Internet is problematical. Schools may already have a computer network, many standalone machines or a mixture of both throughout the school. Different schools use different hardware and software – Apple Macintosh, Acorns, personal computers (PCs).

The technical expertise available within the school will also differ; some schools have a network manager or technician(s) to assist, some depend on the expertise of teaching staff or the local education advisory service. Increasingly, secondary schools are moving towards having networked computers with Internet access either across the whole school or at least in dedicated network rooms or laboratories.

A simple network of computers consists of at least two machines connected together using a cable (*network connection*), with these machines sharing a number of resources, perhaps files, a printer or an Internet connection. A network of this sort is known as a *peer-to-peer network*.

Larger secondary schools require a more advanced network known as a *server-based* network. This gives much more flexibility. A server is a special computer that is not used for anything other than to run the network and typically will be locked away in a cupboard or special room. It acts as a common storage area for files (and often programs) that you want to share on the network. It also enables security so that access can be restricted to authorized persons; this ensures, for example, that sensitive student records are not accessible to pupils.

Hardware and software requirements

Almost any computer can be connected to a network. Different kinds of computers, such as those running Windows and Macintoshes, can exist on the same network and are able to share files with each other.

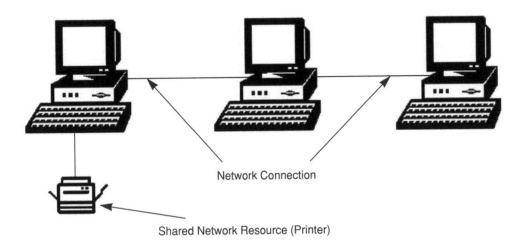

Network Connection

Shared Network Resource (Printer)

A simple computer network. The three PCs can share resources between them, eg access files on the hard disks of other machines and print from the printer attached to the first computer.

Figure 2.1   *A simple network*

Each machine on the network will need to have a network interface card installed and will also need to be configured to connect to a network, although the software to do this is built into the Windows and Macintosh operating systems.

If you require Internet access, you will need to install software such as Web browsers and e-mail programs onto each computer or perhaps load them onto a server so that all users on the network can run them.

Installing networks

Unless you already have a network in your school you will need to get someone to come in and install the nuts and bolts (or rather cables and hubs!) that you need. The following description assumes that you are going to be installing a network using 'UTP' otherwise known as 'category 5' cable (networking people usually talk about 'cat 5'). This cable looks very like telephone cable. Older networks use coaxial cable, which is similar to that used for television aerial cables.

Figure 2.2 shows the main components in a typical network. The hardware used is described in detail in the box proceeding it.

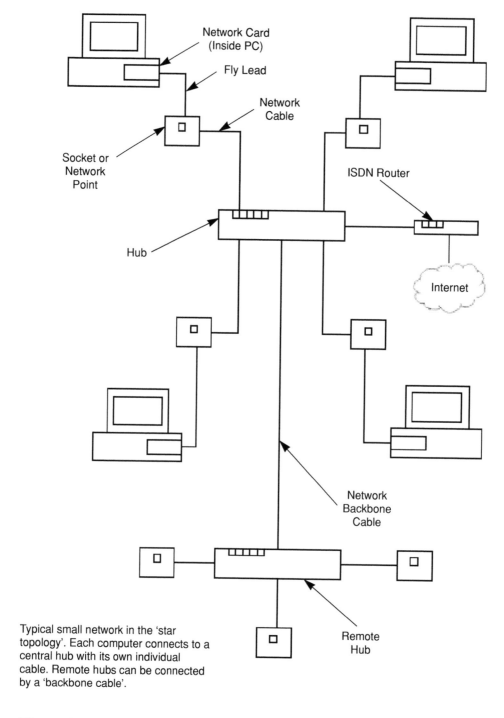

Network Card
(Inside PC)

Fly Lead

Network
Cable

Socket or
Network
Point

ISDN Router

Hub

Internet

Network
Backbone
Cable

Typical small network in the 'star
topology'. Each computer connects to a
central hub with its own individual
cable. Remote hubs can be connected
by a 'backbone cable'.

Remote
Hub

Figure 2.2 *A typical network topology*

The following describes the hardware used in a typical network:

- **Network card (or network interface card, NIC):** Each computer you want to connect to the network needs to have a network card installed in it. Don't worry if your computers do not already have these fitted as they can soon be added. Network cards physically connect the network cabling to the computer.
- **Fly lead (or patch cable):** This lead plugs into the back of the network card and connects it to the socket on the wall. It is very similar to a telephone cable or modem lead.
- **Socket:** Wall sockets, or network points, are where the fly leads are plugged in. These sockets are individually connected to a hub by network cable.
- **Network cable:** The cable is copper wire similar to telephone cable and the most common type installed in new networks is known as 'category 5' or 'UTP' cable, although category 6 cable is now available but is expensive. However, category 5 cable can support very fast networks and can be installed in false ceilings or threaded through ducting depending on the construction of your school.
- **Hub:** Each network socket is connected individually to a hub. Hubs can have somewhere between 4 and 24 sockets connected to them. In larger networks, there will be several hubs all connected together by cable known as a *back-bone*. Sometimes devices known as switches are used instead of hubs; these carry out a similar function but are faster and more expensive! The method of connecting each socket to a central hub is known as a 'star network topology' (see Figure 2.2).
- **Router:** Routers are used to connect more than one network together. In the context of a secondary school, network routers could be used to connect the school network to the Internet, using an ISDN (Integrated Services Digital Network) line, a leased line or ADSL (Asynchronous Digital Subscriber Line) connection.

You will also have to give thought to choosing a server and a *network operating system* (NOS) to run on that server. This is outside the scope of this book, but the two main operating systems used in schools are Windows NT (or Windows 2000) and Novell Netware.

Some suppliers can provide a packaged solution for schools, making it easy to set up and administer the network. As well as installing the server, the other machines on the network, known as *client* machines, will also need to be set up to log on to the server. Users will have to be provided with their own usernames and passwords. This is a big issue for schools in terms of planning, and requires some thought since networks could consist of several hundred machines and even more users.

Locating your computers

One of the main choices that you will have to make is between placing computers at locations all over the school or in dedicated computer rooms or laboratories. Often a combination of the two approaches is the best solution.

In a secondary school, you will almost certainly need to have a number of computers in computer laboratories for teaching purposes. However, your school might also benefit from locating computers in classrooms, the library and staff room. Whatever you decide, try to ensure that all your machines are networked together so that you can share resources and access the Internet. The following tips may help:

- Install far more network sockets than you actually need (this is known as flood wiring) to allow for extra expansion in the future. It will be much cheaper to have these installed when you first install a network rather than adding them later.
- Install sockets in all occupied rooms – classrooms, offices, staff room/s, library, canteen and so forth.
- Try to include administrative staff in the network as well as just teaching staff – make sure the headteacher's office is included!
- Invite more than one networking contractor to visit your site to give you quotations, unless you are planning a small network with a couple of machines or are confident you have the expertise to install the network as a Do It Yourself job.
- Think about where cables and hubs might best be located. Do not leave this totally to the people who actually install the network as they may not be as concerned with the appearance of cables and equipment as you are! You may also wish to specify locking cabinets to prevent children and others accessing the equipment or stealing it.

Connecting your networks

If you want to connect your network to the Internet, there are several ways to do this. If you want to connect more than one machine, something much faster than a simple modem is required. Basically you need a link with more *bandwidth*.

The easiest way to think about bandwidth is to imagine water pipes of different sizes. The bigger the pipe, the more water can travel down it at any one time. The greater the bandwidth, the more data can travel down the link at any one time.

Bandwidth is measured in kbps (kilo bits per second) or Mbps (mega bits per second). A standard modem ranges in speed from 28.8 kbps to 56 kbps, with ISDN giving 64 kbps or 128 kbps. Faster speeds usually require leased line connections that can run at many Mbps (typically 2 Mbps). ADSL (Asynchronous Digital Subscriber Line) is a newer technology offering speeds of up to 2 Mbps at a much cheaper rate than standard leased lines, but is not yet available across the whole United Kingdom.

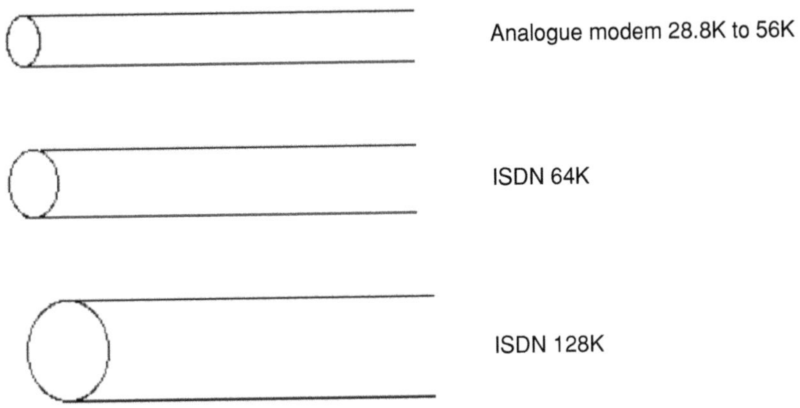

Analogue modem 28.8K to 56K

ISDN 64K

ISDN 128K

Bandwidth available on different sorts of connections to the Internet. The more bandwidth the better! Remember that on a network all computers connected to the network are sharing the bandwidth available on the link to the Internet.

Figure 2.3 *Bandwidth*

The main ways to connect your school network to the Internet are as follows:

● An ISDN line (Integrated Services Digital Network). This is similar to a standard telephone line, in fact it will be delivered in exactly the same way using a pair of copper wires. However, ISDN provides a digital connection. Like a standard phone line, you need to dial up to access the Internet; however, this only takes a second or two compared with around 30 seconds for an analogue modem.

● ISDN offers two telephone channels, each providing a 64 kbps connection. These can be combined together to form a 128 kbps link.

● There are two fees for an ISDN line, a monthly line rental charge for *each channel*, and call charges every time you dial up (also charged per channel). Therefore, a 128 kbps connection is charged at double a 64 kbps. connection. These call charges are at the same rate as voice calls. However, schools are eligible for a special offer where, for a fixed fee, all calls to nominated Internet service providers during term time from 8 am to 6 pm are covered. British Telecommunications (BT) and several cable companies offer this deal. ISDN lines are available in most parts of the country.

● A leased line connection differs from an ISDN line as the connection is always live, in this case, from your school to an Internet service provider. You pay a fixed fee, regardless of how many times you use this live link, where the fee depends on the bandwidth provided and the distance the leased line has to cover. Leased lines are expensive but at least schools can plan their finances in advance since the annual charge is a fixed cost.

- Like ISDN, leased lines can be obtained from BT and the cable companies and are delivered using copper pairs or fibre optic cables depending on the speed of the link.
- ADSL is a new technology currently available only in a few parts of the country, mainly in urban areas such as London and Birmingham. It is similar to a leased line in that it is permanently connected. However, it differs in that it provides a link from your school to your Internet provider via your local telephone exchange, using a standard telephone line. It can be used to make normal voice calls at the same time as accessing the Internet and is significantly cheaper then a leased line. However, your Internet provider must be able to offer ADSL services. The technology cannot be used to provide a network link between buildings.
- The *asynchronous* nature of an ADSL line means that it provides different bandwidth in each direction, that is, it may have a speed of 512 kbps *from* the Internet but only 128 kbps *to* the Internet.

Internet service providers

If you use the Internet at home you will be aware that you need to have an Internet service provider to connect you to the Internet. You can use Freeserve, AOL (America Online), Virgin or any one of several hundred firms providing access. However, when connecting a whole network, although you still need to use an Internet service provider (ISP), you will have fewer services to choose from as you need to select a provider that can support access for a whole network rather than just one machine.

Your LEA (Local Education Authority) may be able to help (see Chapter 3, Other useful tools). Your choice will be further limited if you choose the ISDN connection special offer for schools, as you are then restricted to providers from an approved list of suppliers.

There are many issues you will need to consider when selecting an ISP but do ensure that they can offer firewall protection (see below) for security and/or filtering services (see Chapter 4, Talk! Talk! Talk!) whereby certain potentially unsavoury services, such as online chat, games and UseNet groups, are prevented from reaching the school.

Grids for Learning

As part of the government's strategy to create a National Grid for Learning (NGfL), several local grids for learning have been established. In some areas local grids can offer packaged solutions to connect school networks not only to the wider Internet but perhaps locally to an intranet (see Chapter 3, Other useful tools).

Usually e-mail, filtering and firewalls are provided as part of the package, leaving you to concentrate on your own school network. There may even be financial benefits such as the possibility of linking to the LEA's finance and records systems at the same time.

Firewalls

Leaving all your computers permanently connected to the Internet is risky! Malicious Internet users may try to *hack* into your computers or to gain unauthorized access to sensitive data stored on your network. This is why you need to consider network security very carefully.

A *firewall* sits between your network and the Internet and controls access both in and out of your school network. A firewall can be a dedicated box situated at your site or with your ISP.

Configuring a firewall is a highly specialist skill and unless you are fortunate enough to have that expertise in-house, you would be well advised to ask your ISP to provide suitable firewall services.

Web authoring

So far, we have looked at how we can use the Internet to find information. In particular we have focused on the World Wide Web. We're going to continue to focus on the Web in this section but will be learning how to use the Web to publish information for ourselves. One of the great things about the Internet is that it gives everyone the chance to be a publisher! On the Internet anyone can publish more or less whatever they like.

This part of the book is not going to tell you in full detail how you can author Web pages – this depends a lot on what sort of computer you have and what software you are using. However, it provides some tips to help get you started and pointers to more information. You don't need much to write Web pages for yourself but you will need to be familiar with what the Web is and to have used it yourself for a short while.

HTML and all that!

Don't let anyone tell you that Web pages are 'too hard' for you to do or that you need to be a programmer. Anyone can write Web pages these days! You may hear people talking about a mysterious thing called HTML (HyperText Mark-up Language). This is the language that Web pages are written in and looks something like this:

```
<HTML>

<HEAD>
<TITLE>This is my homepage!!!</TITLE>
</HEAD>

<BODY>
<H1>Welcome to my homepage!!</H1>
<B>This is in Bold!!</B>
<I>And this is in Italics!</I>
</BODY>
```

This 'code' would produce the Web page shown in Figure 2.4.

You might well have noticed that HTML works by putting 'tags' around text that alters the appearance of that text. For example, putting a <B> tag in front of a sentence makes that sentence appear in bold. Placing an end tag </B> after the sentence ensures that the text that follows is no longer in bold.

TIP

You can look at the HTML of a Web page that you have displayed in your browser. In Internet Explorer choose *View* and then *Source*. In Netscape choose *View* and the *Page Source*.

This is quite simple to learn but there is some good news if you are a Windows or a Macintosh user – to write Web pages, you don't need to learn HTML! As you will see in the section 'Hardware and software' below, there are several programs that can write the HTML for you, leaving you to concentrate on the fun bit, designing your pages. Even better, you may already have the software you need on your computer without even knowing it.

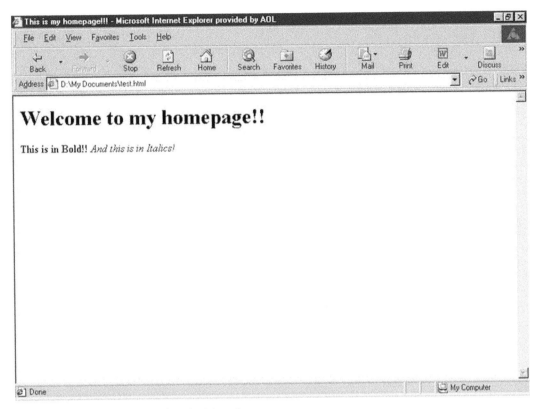

Figure 2.4   *An example of HTML language*

Why bother?

Before you actually start work on your Web site, it's worth considering a few important points to save extra work later on. Ask yourself why you are setting up the Web site. What is its purpose?

Web sites were usually developed because everyone else has one. Historically the first schools to have their own Web sites did so because it was a new thing. The purpose of the site was simple: it was for the sake of having a Web site and because so few schools had Web sites it was a success just to set one up.

The vast majority of secondary schools now have a Web site of some sort. These range from large professionally designed sites to a few unfinished pages. So put some thought into what the Web site will do for your school.

Decide on a plan for your Web site before you start constructing your Web pages. You may wish to sketch it out first by drawing a diagram showing all the links between pages on the site. Think about who will be looking at your pages. Will they be pupils, parents, other teachers, or all of these? Make the pages appropriate to the

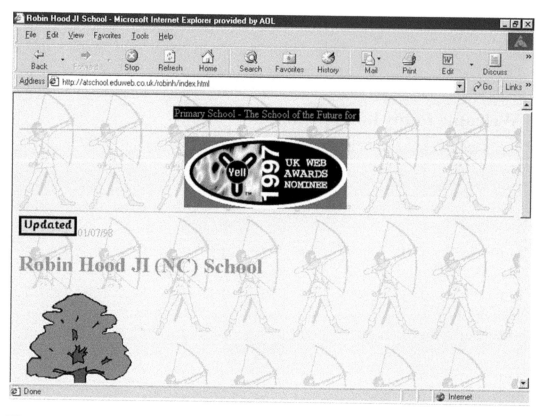

Figure 2.5 *An early school WWW site*

intended audience. You may even want to provide different kinds of content for different audiences.

Parents are now beginning to turn to the Internet as a source of information on education. If they are moving to a new unfamiliar area, they may refer to the Web for information on local schools.

If the first impression a parent and their children have of your school is going to be your Web site, then this is a good reason to put some effort into ensuring that there is plenty of information and even more importantly that it is kept up to date. Nothing is worse than coming to a school Web site with an impressive calendar of events only to find it is from the previous academic year!

Even if you already have a Web site, you may be interested to type your school's name into a search tool and see what you find. Chances are that the first 'hits' will be links to your school's OFSTED (Office for Standard and Testing in Education) report and to DfEE (Department for Education and Employment) performance indicators about your school. These are all freely available and the range of information is slowly growing.

Figure 2.6 *The Web as a marketing tool*

As well as this information about your school from other sources, you may well decide that you would like to provide your own information from a school's point of view. And what's more, information that you make available on your Web site does not have to be for marketing reasons alone.

You may be in the habit of displaying pupils' work on the wall in school, but the Internet makes it possible for work to be seen all over the world. This in itself can be an incentive for achievement. Pupils often work hard when they know that their work is to be published online, particularly if provision is made for any feedback such as using e-mail. You can easily use a scanner or digital camera (see below) to put work onto the school's Web pages.

Key Stage 3 and 4 pupils should be quite able to produce Web pages for themselves after some teaching in the basics of HTML. Using Microsoft Word or Publisher, you should find that producing Web pages is as straightforward as producing a word-processed document to print.

Pupils might put information about their own work and/or interests online or be entrusted to take part in providing the more 'official' information about their school. A

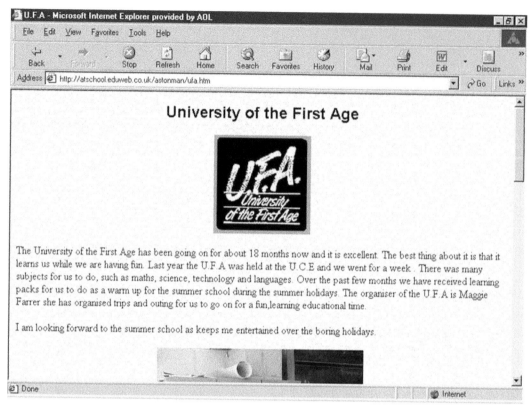

Figure 2.7 *A page produced by a pupil*

professional-looking site created by pupils themselves would make a more impressive site than a 'flash' site designed by a Web design company.

Tools for the job

Hardware and software

You will need a certain amount of hardware and software for Web page authoring. Make sure that you have everything ready before you start.

Unless you already have a Web server at school, you will need to pay for an account with an Internet service provider (ISP). However, the good news is that almost all dial-up Internet service providers such as Research Machines (RM), Demon, Virgin and America On Line (AOL) provide some space for your Web pages on their servers either free or at a nominal fee.

Some hardware and software is required for Web page authoring, as follows:

- **Computer:** You will not need an all-singing, all-dancing, latest-specification computer for constructing simple Web pages. However, Web page work that includes graphics and video requires a computer that has a reasonably fast processor and lots of storage space.
- **Modem or Internet connection:** You will need a modem or networked Internet access.
- **Internet account and Web space:** To publish your Web pages you will need to be able to upload them to the Internet. The method used to do this is referred to as FTP (see Chapter 3, Other Internet tools of the trade). This stores your pages on a Web server that is permanently connected to the Internet.

If you already have an account with them, ask for details, and if you are just setting one up, make sure you check how much space is available. Usually 20 mega bytes (Mb) of space is quite enough.

Many LEAs now provide Web space for schools as part of the local 'Grids for Learning'. An example would be the Birmingham Grid for Learning (http://www.bgfl.org). Often LEAs will provide a school with their own URL (see Chapter 1, Browsing the Web).

Take an imaginary school in Birmingham called 'Newschool', with an ISP; it might have the URL:

http://www.myISP.com/freepages/newschool

But if the URL is provided via the LEA, the school address might be:

http://www.Newschool.bham.sch.uk/

Web authoring software

If you are using a Windows system or a Macintosh, then you probably already have the software you need to create Web pages. Both Microsoft Word and Publisher have built-in Web editing features. Microsoft Word can even save existing Word documents in the HTML format. In Word, all you have to do is choose *File* and then *Save as Web Page* to save a document in HTML. If you intend to use Word for most of your Web authoring, you may want to turn on the special Web authoring toolbars by going to *View* and then clicking on *Toolbars*.

If you are managing a larger Web site with many thousands of pages, then you may need to consider the use of specialist software such as Microsoft FrontPage. This allows you to check hyperlinks (URLs) and update your site more easily.

More advanced professional packages such as Macromedia's Dreamweaver and Authorware can also be used to produce professional sites that contain animation, such as that produced by Flash. Remember though, if you do use Flash, that any individual viewing your site will need the Flash plug-in (see Chapter 3, Other useful tools). Also be careful to pay attention to the download speed when creating advanced sites that rely on large graphics and animations. They can take a long time to download.

There may be courses in your area that could train you in Web design or you may know someone that has already designed Web pages that could help you. Either way, maintaining a professional site takes time and expertise.

Graphics manipulation software

Graphics software is useful to convert Graphics files into the GIF and JPEG formats that are used in Web pages (see Chapter 3, Other Internet tools of the trade). Microsoft Publisher allows you to manipulate images, otherwise you could use shareware programs such as PaintShop Pro (**http://www.jasc.com**).

Graphics programs help you to manipulate images that you already have on your computer or enable you to input an image from a scanner or digital camera. So, for example, you could resize a photograph that you have scanned into your computer in order that it fits in the right place on your Web page.

Scanner

A scanner allows you to scan photographs and drawings into your computer and is very useful for Web page construction. You can scan photographs of the school, pupils, teachers and also any work that the pupils have produced. Scanners are useful for many other things in school.

Make sure you buy a flatbed A4 scanner and check that it will connect to the computer that you are using.

Most scanners available today use either USB (Universal Serial Bus) interfaces or plug into a parallel port (printer port) of a computer. USB scanners are usually the easiest to install and will fit most newer computers (in fact some new machines only have USB ports). If you have an older machine without a USB port, you will need to use a parallel port scanner, and for older Macintosh computers, you will need a SCSI interface scanner.

Digital camera

A digital camera is similar to an ordinary camera but allows you to take a picture and then input it directly into a computer without the need to get the photographs developed or scanned using a scanner, saving time and money. This makes it an excellent teaching and learning tool as images can be incorporated straight into a document without any disruption to the activity.

Digital cameras usually store the pictures they take directly onto a disk or into a memory card that is built into them. This means that to get the pictures onto your computer you have to transfer them in some way. Most cameras have a lead that attaches their storage area to the computer via the serial port or USB port of the computer.

Digital cameras are now much cheaper and of higher quality than previously and are an excellent buy for most schools.

Site design

Most Web sites have a consistent 'look and feel' throughout the whole site. Graphic designers and big companies call this 'corporate identity', but for a school site this might mean all the pages having the same colour background with the school logo on them! Some Web authoring programs allow you to save a page as a 'template' so that all the pages that you base on the template will look the same, that is, have the same colour of text, background colour and so forth. It's worth the time sorting out the basics of site design before you start work as it's much easier to get it right from the first page!

Colour

Think about the colours of your pages. If you do decide to use background images or colours other than plain white, make sure that the text is still legible against the background image and that the link colours are appropriate.

Title

Make sure that each page has a proper title and one that reflects the page's content. The title is important because when you have a site with many pages, you will need to be able to distinguish one from another.

Page ownership

Put your name and the date you last updated information on each page. When typing in dates, it is best to write them out in full (eg 1 May 2001) rather than use shorthand (1/5/01) as this means different things in different countries. If you have one, include an e-mail address on every page so that users can feed back comments about your site.

Contact details

Make sure that at least one page on your site contains full contact details for your school, such as name, address, telephone/fax numbers and e-mail address. It is amazing how many Web sites neglect to include even a telephone number. If a parent was looking at the site and wanted to telephone to arrange a visit, they might be discouraged if they have to ring directory inquiries for a number! When writing phone numbers online, you might want to include them in the international format since some of your site visitors might be calling from outside the UK:

0121 123 1234

becomes:

+44 121 123 1234

It is probably best to include telephone numbers in the local format as well as the international one.

Spelling and other errors

Make sure that you check the document for spelling and other errors before putting it on the Web. This is particularly important for school pages as it looks dreadful to potential parents and visitors if words are spelt incorrectly, and the mistakes might even make for an interesting article in the local papers.

Speed of access

Remember that many people still use slow modems to access the Web so huge graphics and lots of the latest bells and whistles may look good on your machine but not so good on an old machine using an old modem!

Browsers

Though the HTML language is supposed to be a standard, the two main browsers, *Microsoft Internet Explorer* and *Netscape Navigator*, often display the same page in slightly different ways. This situation is further complicated by the fact that different versions of the same browser, that is, Netscape 4.0 and Netscape 4.5, may display the same page differently.

It is a good idea, therefore, to try viewing your Web site in both of these browsers and in different versions so that you can see the image that potential visitors to your site might experience.

Page size

Screen resolution is measured in 'pixels' which are just dots of light on a screen. Most 14-inch monitors are set to work on 640 × 480 pixels; most 15-inch monitors work at 800 × 600 pixels. The screen resolution affects the size of images on the screen and how much information you can see at once. In general, design your pages to work at 800 × 600 screen resolution with at least 256 colours. You may also like to check images at a lower screen resolution (eg 640 × 480) to see if they work.

Screen length

Avoid pages that are longer than two to three computer screens in length. Divide a long page into more manageable 'chunks' and put links to these pages from your very first page – known as the Home Page.

Using graphics

Size of graphics

Web pages look good with graphics on them, but there are a few tips that will help to ensure that the graphics do not deter visitors from reading the page. This can happen when they take forever to download, thus spoiling the effect.

Avoid huge graphics files, or if you want to include them, use 'thumbnails'. Thumbnails are simply smaller versions of a larger graphic that are displayed by the browser in place of the larger image. They can be created in a graphics package (see 'Graphics software' above) by resizing the image.

The smaller 'thumbnail' images are then made into clickable links to their larger versions and give the user an idea of what the images are like before downloading them. In general, graphics should be no larger than 40–50 kbps (kilobytes).

GIFs and JPEGs

Try to use the GIF file format for line drawings and the JPEG file format for photographs. GIFs and JPEGs are just different sorts of graphic file formats that use compression to reduce their size (see Chapter 3, Other Internet tools of the trade). For example, an image of say 100 kbps can be reduced in size by compression to about 30 kbps. The main advantage of using compression is to reduce the overall size of Web documents so that they download much faster.

Progressive loading of graphics

When given the option, save GIF and JPEG files in 'interlaced' or 'progressive' file formats using a graphics package. This means that the viewer will see the image

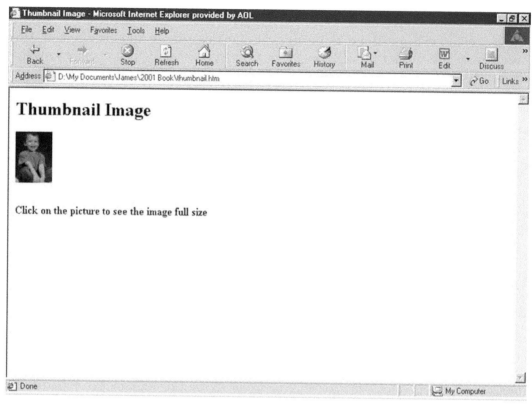

Figure 2.8 *Thumbnail image*

emerging bit by bit as the graphic downloads. Otherwise, you will have to wait until the whole image is downloaded to the screen before viewing it.

Width of images

Make sure the width of graphics files fit into the 640 × 480 screen resolution that many people still use. Set your monitor's screen resolution to these settings and check out your pages before making them available to your intended users for viewing.

ALT tag

The ALT tag is part of HTML script and consists of words that are displayed by the browser as an alternative to the graphic itself. Therefore, if the image fails to display, you can still see a description of it. If you wrote the following HTML:

IMG SRC='happy.gif' ALT='Picture of Smiling Face'

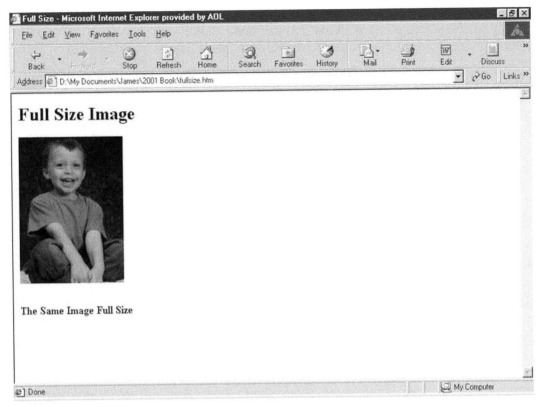

Figure 2.9 *Larger version of thumbnail image*

and your image failed to display on the Web page, you would see 'Picture of Smiling Face' appear on the screen in place of the image.

It is a good idea to go to the trouble of using the ALT tag to insert a meaningful description of any images you are using. Some of the users that access the Web using text browsers can only 'read' the ALT tags and cannot view images.

Where to find graphics

As well as images that you scan or produce yourself, you might also want to use ready-made graphics on your Web site. Whenever using an image produced by someone else, pay special attention to copyright (see Copyright below). There are several sites on the Web that exist just to provide graphics for Web sites. You can find these by using a search tool or visit the site:

http://www.clipart.com

This site contains links to many sources of either free clipart or ones for which you pay a small fee. You may also be able to buy images on CD ROM, but again be very careful to check that you are allowed to use these online.

For more help on downloading from the Web, see Chapter 1 in this book.

Animated GIFs

You may sometimes find pages that have animated graphics on them. These are usually 'animated GIFs'. If you would like to use simple animation on your pages, then you can create your own using a specialized program or, alternatively, download ready-made animated GIFs from the Web.

Do a search using the keywords 'animated GIF' in a search tool (see Chapter 3, Seek and ye shall find) and download the GIFs to your computer, as described in Chapter 1.

Links

When the World Wide Web first started, it was based on the idea of hypertext links, those underlined words that can be clicked on and which then lead to other Web pages. Nowadays, it's not only words that act as hyperlinks. You can enable graphics and a variety of navigational aids, such as forward and backward buttons, to lead to other Web pages. Whatever you do, try to place a link back to your Home page on every page on your Web site.

When creating links to another site or within your own site, check that the links actually work and keep checking them at regular intervals, as any future alterations may cause the links to stop working. Certain Web page authoring programs (such as *Microsoft FrontPage*) can check all the links between pages on your site, and even links on your pages to other people's Web sites.

However, avoid including too many hyperlinks to other people's sites on your pages as users might jump straight off to these and never return! Many sites avoid this problem by concentrating all external links together on a single 'links' page.

Updating

Remember that people will find your site boring if it never changes. Keep it up to date! In particular, if the site promises newsletters or other similar items then make sure these are actually added. People will not appreciate seeing news concerned with the Spring term at the end of the Summer term. If you need to keep 'old' information because some of it is still relevant, then plan for part of your site to act as an archive.

It might also help to have a 'What's New' page so that regular visitors to your site can quickly see what has changed since their last visit. As mentioned before, always check your links to ensure that they are still working.

Making it interactive

When Web pages were first invented, they often consisted of just plain text files with a few hypertext links. However, it was not long before graphics were added and now most Web sites make use of both text and graphics to make the content more interesting and easier to navigate. One of the great things about the Web now is that you can encourage interaction.

For example, you can send an e-mail message to the author of a page, fill out an online form, or even complete a test and have your score displayed online almost immediately.

The latest Web sites are making use of sound and video to enhance the presentation of the pages. In fact, it is even possible to 'Webcast' live events, such as concerts, and to listen to radio stations. When sounds and video were first added to Web pages they were often in a format specific to certain types of computers, that is, .WAV files for Windows or .QT files for the Macintosh (see Chapter 3, Other Internet tools of the trade). These had to be downloaded to the computer before the sound or video could be played.

Recently, technology known as 'streaming' has been introduced which means that sound and video can be heard or seen as it is being downloaded to the computer. A disadvantage is that, in addition to needing a sound card and either speakers or headphones attached to your computer, you must have additional software such as Real Player or Windows Media Player on your machine.

Fortunately, the latest Web browsers often have Real Player or Windows Media Player installed for you, but if your browser does not, then you can download the plug-in by visiting the following sites:

http://www.real.com

http://www.windows.com/ie

Copyright

Many people think that the usual rules of copyright do not apply on the Internet, but this is not the case. When producing pages, it is essential to ensure that you either own the copyright to the material you are publishing yourself or that you have obtained the consent of the copyright owners before publishing it.

It is important to remember that images you may see on other people's pages cannot just be copied and used on your page without consent. In fact, in some cases, even the owner of the site from which you downloaded the resources may not have permission to use them! Be vigilant!

There are some sites that specifically allow you to download and use their resources on your pages; however, sometimes they ask you to put a link and/or a credit to them on your pages. You should always do this when asked. You should proceed as if publishing the document in more conventional formats and not let the ease of downloading and copying other people's files from the Internet get you into trouble online!

Responsibility for Web page content

It is usual for a school to appoint one person to be in overall charge of the Web site. This ensures that there is consistency in the look and content of all the pages. It would be wise to get the permission of the headteacher before starting work on a site and to ensure that he or she sees the pages before they are published. Some schools have formed small working groups to provide and update content on their pages.

It is particularly important if you are allowing pupils to create Web content to check its suitability for public viewing before publishing it online. Remember that people will judge your school from the content of its Web pages.

Child protection

When using pictures of pupils on Web sites, you may wish to obtain the consent of parents in advance if this is something that the school would normally do when publishing pupils' photographs elsewhere.

It is sensible not to include the full name of a child or any other information that might identify an individual pupil. If pupils maintain their own personal Web pages and are including photographs of themselves, ensure that they avoid revealing their full names or any other personal details online. Encourage them to use first names only. Always practise caution. A number of schools only allow pictures of groups of pupils together and avoid the mention of any names altogether.

If your site offers the facility for visitors to send e-mail messages directly to a pupil or group of pupils, then it is important to make sure that a teacher checks their content. It is better to be safe than sorry where a pupil's online safety is concerned. Remind pupils that people are not always who they claim to be online. More information about these issues can be found in Chapter 4 of this book when talking about collaborative working.

Getting your Web files onto the Internet

One of the most confusing parts of publishing a Web site is the process of transferring the Web files that you have produced on your own computer to a Web server (computer). The Web server might be that of your Internet service provider or one maintained at your own school. You do this using a process known as File Transport Protocol (FTP) (see Chapter 3, Other Internet tools of the trade).

In order to connect to your Web server, you will need to know some basic information such as the Internet address of the Web server, and a username and password provided to you by the Web server administrator. This is sometimes the same as the one you have for e-mail and logging onto the Internet, but you would need to check this with your ISP or, again, with your Web server administrator. Once you have uploaded your files onto the Web server, check that they all work correctly by using your Web browser to go to the Internet address of your pages.

Adding your pages to search engines

Having published your pages on the Internet, remember that unless you do something about it, no one will know that they are there or where to find them. It's a bit like having a new telephone line connected. Until you tell people the number or list it in a directory, no one will know it is there!

All the major search engines have pages where you can submit a new Internet address. You can usually find these on the Home page of the relevant search tools. You can find a list of search sites in Chapter 3.

Don't forget to include the Web site address of your school on letterheads, newsletters and other hard-copy correspondence.

Resources

Networks:
Ingram, Peter *Networking in Easy Steps*, Computer Steps

ISDN:
http://www.bt.com/isdn/index.html

http://www.seg.co.uk/

http://www.aa.nu/

ADSL:
http://www.btopenworld.com/

uk.telecom:
Usenet newsgroup is a valuable source of information on ISDN and ADSL

Using the Web in schools

The Web itself is a great place to look for information on Web page authoring. Use a search tool to look for the keyword 'HTML'. Some of the following links might be useful.

A Beginner's Guide to HTML:
http://www.ncsa.uiuc.edu/General/Internet/WWW/HTMLPrimer.html

Bare Bones guide to HTML:
http://werbach.com/barebones/

Craig's 1 stop for HTML:
http://www.cyber-quest.com/home/craig/index.html

HTML Crash Course:
http://www.w3-tech.com/crash/

HTML made really easy:
http://www.jmarshall.com/easy/html/

HTML: An interactive tutorial for beginners:
http://www.davesite.com/webstation/html/

Teach Me! HTML:
http://www.geocities.com/Athens/Forum/4977/index.html

3

Common Internet facilities

Seek and ye shall find

One of the most infuriating features of the Internet is the difficulty in finding the information you want. Imagine searching for information in the world's largest library, where all the books have no covers or title, are not stored in any particular order, and are not indexed in a central catalogue. All right, so this isn't quite the same situation as we have on the Internet at present, but it's close!

In response to this problem, the past few years has seen a growth in search tools, some of which organize Internet resources into searchable subject areas, some of which keyword-search documents and others which deliver personalized information to your desktop. If you want to save yourself time and effort, it helps if you learn how to make best use of the available search tools. Used correctly, they are a great support in reaching the information you require as quickly and effectively as possible.

However, regardless of the search tool being used, it is far more important to have an effective search strategy. This is true regardless of the type of electronic information you are searching through, whether it is a CD ROM, library database or the vastness of the Web.

The first step in any information search is to analyse the subject you're seeking. When you're looking for something, it helps to know what it is. Sounds obvious, but there are times when we've all tried to search the Web with only a vague idea of what we're looking for.

Developing your search skills:

1. Be clear on exactly what you're looking for. If you're not too sure, use a subject directory first.

2. Think of more than one word that best describes the subject.
3. Be prepared to revise your search words if the first results are not what you wanted.
4. Evaluate what you find.
5. Stay focused.

For example, we want to find out about Shakespeare. Fine! Do we mean we want to learn about the playwright known as Shakespeare? Or maybe we want to find out what literature he produced? Or view a particular Shakespearean piece? On the other hand, we might want to trace the linguistic origins of the language Shakespeare used. What *exactly* do we want to know?

The most important thing to remember about Internet and Web search tools is that they are constantly evolving. No sooner do you think you've got to know a particular search tool than suddenly its facilities change. In fact, that's true of the Internet generally. It's a dynamic system where information is added and removed regularly. This can be both annoying and exciting! So just bear this in mind whilst you're reading the following section on search tools.

Getting the best from the search tools

There is no search tool that has an index to the entire contents of the Internet. Each search site uses different search techniques and builds its index in a different way. These tools use software known as spiders or robots to trawl and index the Web and you'll find that some index every word on every Web page, whereas others only index the headings, subheadings or hypertext links on a page.

Usually the bigger the size of the database being searched, the greater the number of hits you receive, but you might still find that these results are not very useful or relevant. Therefore, the way the software ranks the results is very important. A good, solid results ranking will hopefully mean you'll only need to look at the first 10 or 20 hits.

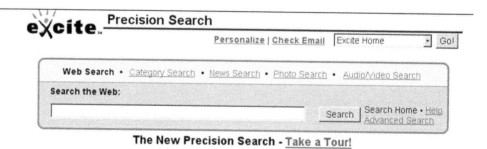

Figure 3.1 *The Excite search site*

Given all these variables, it might be a good idea to use more than one search site to find the information you're looking for. You'll be surprised at how different the results can be for the same search, using the same words, but using different tools. Try it and see!

Tricks of the trade

Search sites are getting better all the time but it helps if you speak their language. This means knowing about things called Boolean Operators and wildcards.

What's Boolean?

We don't want to confuse matters too much but certain words, referred to as Boolean Operators, are such useful things that we really couldn't talk about successful searches without mentioning at least the most common ones: AND, OR, NOT and combinations of these. Boolean operators enable you to make your search more specific by looking for certain words whilst ignoring others.

A number of search tools will accept Boolean Operators written in capital letters alone, others will accept them in lower case. Check out the help and tips section of the search site you're using. It will save time in the long run.

Boolean AND: enables you to search documents that contain two keywords.
Example:
kids AND software
should produce results that contain BOTH the word 'software' and the word 'kids'.

    Boolean OR: broadens your search to include ANY of the keywords. This is useful for alternative spellings.
Example:
counseling OR counselling
    Boolean NOT: narrows your search by excluding one meaning of a word.
Example:
alien AND NOT immigrant
(Note that sometimes you cannot use NOT on its own.)

Wildcards

In addition, some engines allow you to use a symbol as a wildcard. You can substitute these symbols for a letter or number or for a set of letters or numbers in a search. The most common symbols are the star *, and the hash #, but you might find others in use.

Example:

educat*

should instruct the search engine to look for words starting with 'educat', such as: education, educational, educated.

Top tips for searching the Web:

1. Think about your task before rushing to use a search tool. If you know what general category the information is related to, you can use one of the subject-based tools like Yahoo. Go directly to the topic you think will contain the information you want and see if you find it there. If you are searching for a specific name, use a tool like Alta Vista that searches by keywords, that is, responds to one or more words you type in.

2. If you are aware the information you are seeking has several characteristics, such as geographical location or related history, you may find you will need to perform more than one search cycle, refining your search criteria each time round.

3. Commonly used words (such as back, up, from) make poor search keywords. The more distinctive a word, the more useful it will be.

4. Use more than one search site. Every search tool indexes in a different manner. A keyword may work well with one tool, and badly with another. Try to understand how the keywords you specify relate to the results so with time you can work out how the tool searches.

5. Wildcards are symbols that can represent any character or group of characters in a word. They are useful for retrieving words with different spellings and/or words with a common root (eg flower, flowering, flowered). Symbols used to represent a wildcard vary from one search engine to another, the most common ones being *, #, and ?. For example, to find centre and center, you could search for cent**.

6. If your search produces no results, ensure you've read the tool's help facility, make sure the spelling is right, and if the search tool permits, use Boolean Operators. Boolean Operators enable you to make your search more specific by allowing you to look for certain words whilst ignoring others (see section on Boolean Operators). They are represented by the words AND, OR and NOT. If you still get no results, try to be less specific in your query and use variations on words. If even this fails, use another search site.

7. If your search produces too many results, try again using words that are more unique to what you're looking for. Think of words related to the information you're seeking. Again, search tools that support Boolean logic might be useful here.

---

8. Bookmark your results page if you think you will be returning to it more than once. Or save it as a source file on your local hard disk or personal area on the server.

9. If you're receiving error messages or cannot make a connection at all, the server may be too busy or temporarily down. Try again after a couple of minutes or wait until a less busy time of the day. Remember to take advantage of world time zones, and use a search site when its local time is not a busy period.

10. If you get an error message stating that the file cannot be found, that link may no longer exist or the address may have changed. The Internet is dynamic and constantly changing so you may find this is a common occurrence.

Other ways of finding information

In addition to using search sites, you can also save yourself a great deal of time by making use of the educational links gathered by other educators. Take a look at the British Broadcasting Corporation's (BBC) Educational links (http://www.bbc.co.uk/plsql/education/home/), Norfolk Local Education Authority (http://www.norfolk.gov.uk/education/default.htm) and the Virtual Teacher Centre's Curriculum resources (http://vtc.ngfl.gov.uk). In addition, a number of the local Grids for Learning and some school Web sites contain a collection of educationally relevant links. There are also sites such as that of SchoolsNet (http://www.schoolsnet.com) which contain a library of many thousands of validated links.

Resources – search sites

The following search tools are divided into five main types:

- subject directories;
- search tools;
- meta search sites;
- specialized search sites;
- UK search sites.

Subject directories

Subject directories are hierarchically organized indexes categorized into subject areas. They are usually compiled by humans, or have some human intervention, and many include a search facility to enable you to search the categories. For a broad topic, use one of these subject directories first; for more specific information, try one of the search tools that uses keywords and/or Boolean Operators.

The first starting place is the Argus Clearinghouse, which offers a guide to many of these specialized directories:

Argus Clearinghouse:
http://www.clearinghouse.net/

Examples of subject specific directories are:

Yahoo
http://www.yahoo.com/

Galaxy
http://galaxy.tradewave.com/

Internet Public Library
http://www.ipl.org/ref/

World Wide Web Virtual Library
http://vlib.org

Magellan
http://www.mckinley.com/

The Otis Index
http://www.otis.net/index.html

Search.com
http://www.search.com/

Search tools

Search tools are best used for conducting keyword searches (searches that contain one or more words). Each differs in its search speed, interface, display of results, and the amount of help it offers. These sites also differ in the manner in which they search.

Examples:

Alta Vista
http://altavista.digital.com/

Ask Jeeves
http://www.askjeeves.com

EuroFerret
http://www.webtop.com/search/topferret?PAGE=search&LOOK=euroferret

Excite
http://www.excite.com/

G.O.D
http://www.god.co.uk/

HotBot
http://www.hotbot.com/

Infoseek
http://www.infoseek.com/

Lycos
http://www.lycos.com/

OpenText
http://search.opentext.com/

REX
http://rex.skyline.net/

WebCrawler
http://webcrawler.com/

Meta search sites

These search sites allow you to search multiple databases simultaneously, via a single interface. There are also sites available that collect the different search tools in one place. They do not always offer the same level of control over the search as the individual search tools, but their response time can be fast.

Many meta sites can now sort results by site and type of resource, and some allow you to decide which search tools to include.

Examples:

Aesir
http://www.aesir.com/aesir/staff/JimSearch.html

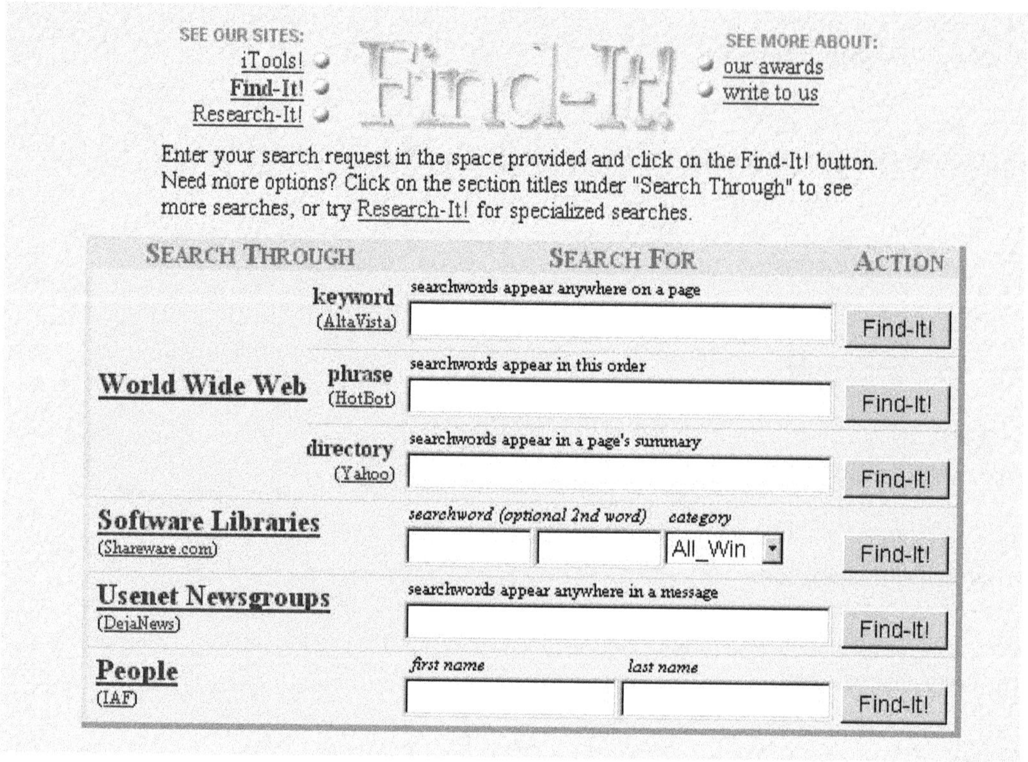

Figure 3.2   *The Find-It meta search site*

All 4 One
http://all4one.com/

Dogpile
http://www.dogpile.com/

Find-It
http://www.itools.com/find-it/find-it.html

Google
http://www.google.com

Meta Crawler
http://www.metacrawler.com/

Search.com
http://www.search.com

Specialized search sites

These are search sites that cater for very specific subject areas or specialist groups.

Figure 3.3 *The Yahooligans site for kids*

You can find more specialized UK-based search facilities below (UK search sites):

Achoo – healthcare
http://www.achoo.com/

Aqueous – water related
http://www.aqueous.com/

Ask Jeeves for Kids – a search facility for children
http://www.ajkids.com/

BigBook – US businesses
http://www.bigbook.com/

Cinemachine – movie reviews
http://www.cinemachine.com

Deja News
http://www.deja.com/

Shareware – software
http://www.shareware.com/

Yahooligans – a search site for children
http://www.yahooligans.com/

UK search sites

Since it can be quicker for users in the United Kingdom (UK) to access sites in the UK, here is a list of search engines, divided into the subject directories, search engines and specialized tools.

Examples:

Alta Vista UK – generic tool
http://uk.altavista.com/

Ask Jeeves UK – generic tool
http://www.ask.co.uk/

Excite – UK
http://uk.excite.com/

Lycos-UK
http://www-uk.lycos.com/

Yahoo UK – generic tool
http://www.yahoo.co.uk

Yellow Pages UK – organizational searches
http://www.yell.co.uk/

ADAM – architecture, design and media
http://www.adam.ac.uk/

EEVL – Edinburgh Engineering Virtual Library
http://eevl.ac.uk/

OMNI – Medical
http://omni.ac.uk/

SOSIG – Social sciences
http://sosig.esrc.bris.ac.uk/

Additional resources – searching

Barlow, Linda (February 1997) The Spider's Apprentice – Tips on Searching the Web:
http://www.monash.com/spidap.html

Evaluation of selected Internet search tools (January 1997):
http://www.library.nwu.edu/resources/internet/search/evaluate.html

Notess, Greg R (February 1997) 'Comparing Net Directories', Database 20.1 61–64:
http://www.onlineinc.com/database/FebDB97/nets2.html

Sullivan, Danny (January 1997) A Webmaster's Guide to Search Engines and Directories:
http://calafia.com/webmasters/

Tillman, Hope N (February 1997) Evaluating Quality on the Net:
http://www.tiac.net/users/hope/findqual.html

LibrarySpot's Search Engine Tips:
http://www.libraryspot.com/features/searchenginetips.htm?news

Other useful tools

Personalized pages

Internet and Web developers are always looking for easier ways of delivering the information you want to your desktop. Many sites now offer personalized Web pages that are customized and intended to save you time and effort.

Search tools such as Yahoo, Excite and Ask Jeeves lead the way in the field of personalized Web pages, although there are other examples.

My Yahoo is one example of an extensive customized Web site that can be altered to reflect your tastes. Just answer a few questions about your lifestyle – music, recreation, shopping and other interests, and from then on, whenever you go to the My Yahoo site, only information pertaining to your interests are displayed. This type of personalization still requires you to make the effort to link to the relevant Web site and sometimes requires you to login with your own username and password.

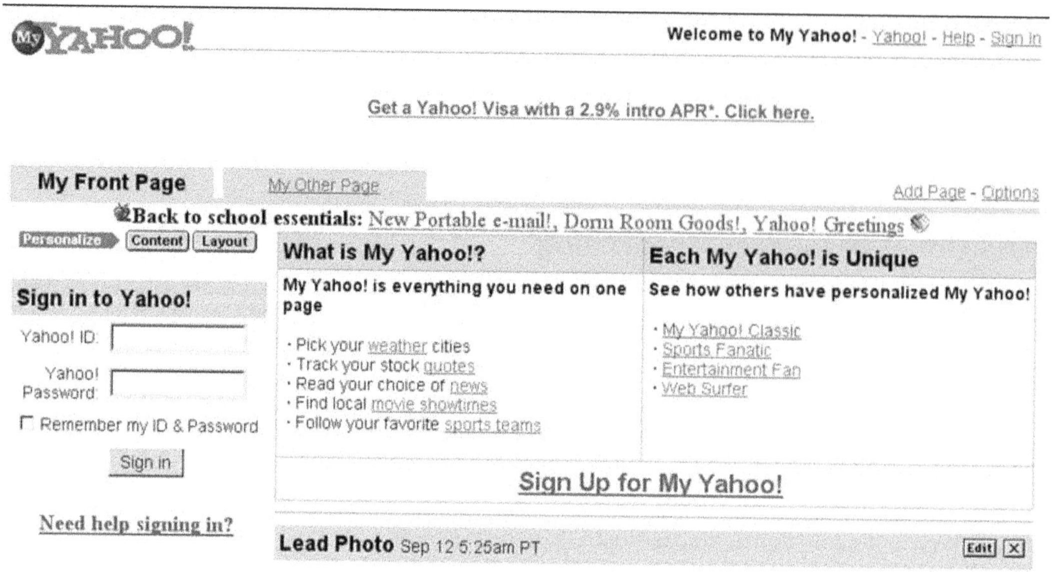

Figure 3.4 *My Yahoo customized Web site*

The idea of personalizing information extends to the use of Web-based e-mail, where you can set up e-mail lists on the Web. These sites offer you your very own personalized Home Page where all your groups are listed and where you can access your 'account' details to amend and change your e-mail group details online (see Chapter 4, So how do you do it?).

Resources – personalized pages

Ask Jeeves:
http://www.askjeeves.com/

Excite:
http://www.excite.com/search/

My Yahoo:
http://my.yahoo.com

Cookies

Personalized sites and other Web sites that depend on knowing who you are in order for you to make use of their facilities use something called 'cookies'. Cookies are files that a Web site copies to your hard disk when you connect to it. This file, or cookie, contains information about you or rather it contains links to a database that is connected to the Web server that sent you the cookie. The sort of information it might contain includes passwords, lists of pages you've visited, and the date when you last looked at a certain Web page

For example, if you shop for books online, the bookstore's Web site might use a cookie to store information about your favourite book titles, and later use that information to recommend particular books.

You can choose to switch off the cookies facility if you object to sites copying files to your computer and holding information about you, but if you do so, many sites that depend on them to identify you may not work properly. You can find out whether you have any cookies by doing a search on your machine for a file called *cookies.txt* or *MagicCookie* if you use a Macintosh computer. You should be able to open these files using any text or word processing software.

Resources – cookies

A Frequently Asked Questions (FAQ) file about security and cookies:
http://www.w3.org/Security/Faq/wwwsf7.html

Cookies Central:
http://www.cookiecentral.com/

Plug-ins

Web browsers are capable of doing more than just displaying text and graphics. You can also display animation, sound and video. However, to do this, you may need to download a special program that works with your Web browser. These are often referred to as *plug-ins.*

Often a site will tell you that, to view their video or listen to their audio files, you need a particular plug-in and will give a pointer to a location where you can download that plug-in.

To install a plug-in, just follow the instructions on downloading (see Other useful tools, below). Plug-ins will be required to complete some of the activities in the curriculum section of this book.

Some of the more common plug-ins are detailed below, together with the site from which you can download them. The latest versions of some Web browsers have the most popular plug-ins already installed.

Director Shockwave and Flash

Macromedia Shockwave Player and Macromedia Flash Player are both free multimedia viewers from Macromedia. Shockwave is produced using Shockwave Director and can display graphics, sound, animation, text and video. It is a powerful, generic multimedia tool with many features.

Macromedia Flash is used to produce vector graphics and animation (see Other Internet tools of the trade, below) and does not contain as many features as Shockwave Director. Web designers use Flash to create and deliver low-bandwidth Web sites. The Flash Player is automatically included with any download of the Shockwave Player.

Resources – plug-ins

Shockwave and Flash:
http://www.macromedia.com

List of plug-ins for Netscape:
http://www.phoenixat.com/scott/plugins.html

Examples of Flash on the Web:

Channel 4's *Big Brother* programme
http://www.bigbrother.terra.com/

Disney
http://www.disney.com

The Brain Girl
http://www.thebraingirl.com/

Examples of Shockwave on the Web:

Stressfree Travel's Travel Games
http://www.stressfree-travel.com/

Tango's Repent Game
http://www.positive-internet.com/~deep/repent/

Adobe Acrobat Reader

Acrobat lets you view documents with the original formats intact. This is often used for instruction manuals or government publications. The DfEE (The Department for Education and Employment) have used this format to make inspection reports on schools available on the Internet.

Resources – Adobe

Download the Adobe Acrobat from:
http://www.adobe.com/

View the Inspection Reports at:
http://www.ofsted.gov.uk/inspect/index.htm

Real Player

Real Player allows you to experience live audio and video broadcasts (called *Webcasts*) and also listen to and watch audio/video files as they download rather than having to wait until the files are on your computer to play them. This facility to listen and view files before they are fully downloaded is referred to as the 'streaming' of media. Basically, streaming media is a method of making audio, video and other multimedia available in real time over the Internet or intranets, with no file to take up space on your hard disk.

Resources – Real Player

Download Real Player from:

http://www.real.co.uk
http://www.real.com

Example of Real Player – Channel 4's *Big Brother* programme:

http://www.bigbrother.terra.com/

QuickTime

Some sites use QuickTime to display multimedia files and experience Webcasts created for QuickTime. QuickTime was originally a multimedia product for the Macintosh computer but is now also available for Windows users. The latest version of the QuickTime Pro player handles video, sound, animation, graphics, text, music, and even three-dimensional movies and imagery.

Resources – QuickTime

Tucows – for a selection of plugins:
http://tucows.rmplc.co.uk/

Download QuickTime from:

http://www.quicktime.apple.com

View examples of QuickTime use in learning at:

http://www.apple.com/quicktime/qtv/learning/

Virtual Tour of The Louvre Museum:

http://www.louvre.or.jp/louvre/QTVR/anglais/index.htm

Offline browsing

To save time, money and to accommodate classrooms that do not have a connection to the Internet, it is possible to save Web pages onto a disk or server. This is known as *offline* browsing. Using dedicated software, you can specify what pages you want and leave the computer to download them. The files will be saved to your hard disk and you can then open them in your Web browser and browse through them.

If you find a *hyperlink* that points to a site other than the one you have downloaded, you will not be able to follow that link, but otherwise the process works just like being online. Another advantage is that the pages will appear much faster.

You can obtain sophisticated offline programs that can download a whole Web site to your local hard disk for you to use later. Teleport Pro is available for PC users, WebWhacker for the Macintosh. Acorn users can obtain SiteSeer or WebTool.

Offline browsing has become more and more difficult to achieve in recent years since many Web sites are now starting to use databases for storing information and then simply display this information via the Web. These 'database-driven' sites cannot be downloaded easily, if at all, using offline programs.

Resources – working offline

Teleport (Windows):
http://www.tenmax.com

WebWhacker (Macintosh and Windows):
http://www.bluesquirrel.com/whacker

SiteSeer (Acorn):
http://www.arsvcs.demon.co.uk/r-comp/index.html

WebTool (Acorn):
http://www.argonet.co.uk/products.html

Intranets

Commercial companies and many educational institutions, particularly colleges of further education and universities, have built whole internal networks based on Internet technology. These internal networks are called intranets.

Since Web browsers work on any computer, whether they are a personal computer (PC), a Macintosh or an Acorn, setting up an intranet allows every individual with a browser on their computer to add to or use the information stored on it, provided that they have permission to access the system.

All documents can be converted to a Web format or accessed using the Web. House memos, staff telephone numbers, school policies, the school ICT (information and communications technology) strategic plan, learning materials, assessments, in fact, whatever you wanted to hold centrally could be converted so that you can view it via a Web browser.

A number of schools have now developed a public Web site, open to everyone via the Net, alongside a closed intranet site, open only to their pupils and staff.

Resources – intranets

The Complete Intranet Resource:
http://www.intrack.com/intranet/index.shtml

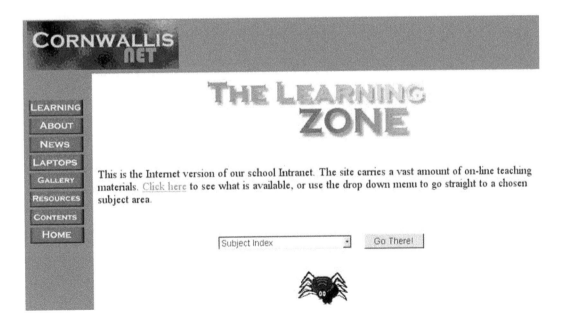

Figure 3.5   *Example of a school Web site reflecting the school intranet*

The Intranet/Extranet Research Centre:
http://www.cio.com/forums/intranet/

Extranets

Whereas an intranet is usually only accessible to people who are members of the same school, an extranet provides various levels of accessibility to individuals from outside the school. You can access an extranet only if you have a valid username and password, and your identity determines which parts of the extranet you can view.

Resources – extranets

Complete Intranet Resource's guide to Extranets:
http://www.intrack.com/intranet/extra.shtml

The Intranet/Extranet Research Centre:
http://www.cio.com/forums/intranet/

The virtual classroom

With the advent of the Internet, there has been much talk about how learning can now be delivered at a distance, with no need for individuals necessarily to attend face-to-face courses. It is suggested that the Internet has the potential to open up learning to a wider audience by allowing a person to have greater flexibility regarding where, when and how they learn. This concept is often referred to in education as the virtual classroom, virtual university, or virtual learning environment.

There are two main types of computer-based systems available to deliver and track learning material. First, you can find systems that provide their own content, are virtually closed to external third-party products, and are delivered via their own multimedia interface, either via the Web or on a stand-alone machine or an internal computer network. These systems include integrated learning systems (ILS), in which the software installs and delivers content whilst also monitoring, tracking and reporting on the progress a pupil makes through that content.

Second, there are systems that are 'shells' for your own content, that can launch and run any third-party products, and also be used to develop your intranet and school Web site. Manufacturers may refer to both types as managed or virtual learning environments (MLEs or VLEs). However, M/VLEs tend to have certain features in common, and these include:

● a password security and user profiling facility;
● the ability to deliver and manage course materials;
● the ability to deliver and manage classes and groups;

- a pupil tracking and assessment facility;
- a number of communications facilities such as e-mail, discussion groups, bulletin boards and online chat;
- the ability to change (configure) the look and functions of the system to which pupils have access.

The potential of the school extranet to open up the curriculum to pupils who cannot necessarily attend school full-time is now a real possibility. Schools can allow pupils access to electronic resources, lesson content, communications facilities (see Chapter 2) and management tools – all of which can come together to support learners remotely.

An example of the potential of online education can be viewed on the Web site *digitalbrain*. The site contains content covering the UK National Curriculum for ages 7–16 years plus a number of post-16 courses. Any learner can personalize their online area (see Personalized pages above), store their work and files online, share projects and ideas, schedule online events and collaborate with other learners and teachers using e-mail and chat (see Chapter 4). Many of the facilities on offer on this Web site can be offered by a school so that the same levels of service are offered via the school intranet, extranet or managed/virtual learning environment (see Other useful tools, below). All you need is the appropriate technical expertise.

The advantages of placing some or all of the course materials online include the ability to:

- alter and amend materials quickly and easily – it is cheaper to amend the electronic rather than hard copies of materials;
- add new content when required;
- provide different paths through the material;
- allow pupils to work through materials at their own pace;
- enable pupils to repeat areas of difficulty;
- track and report on progress through materials.

The disadvantages of online learning are that it:

- cannot fully replace face-to-face delivery. Despite best attempts, it cannot replicate the formal and informal benefits that everyday contact with teachers and other pupils affords;
- requires regular access to a computer and often to the Internet;
- requires a basic level of information technology skills;
- is expensive to deliver. In order to be effective, materials need to be designed for online delivery. Good online learning relies on engaging pupils. In addition, pupils still require a great deal of support by teachers and tutors, whether this support is delivered electronically or face-to-face.

Online courses do not have to be aimed at pupils alone. Some schools are starting to consider online delivery as a mechanism to facilitate staff development. The New Opportunities Fund (NOF) training for practising teachers can contribute to some of the costs required to support the training of school staff and librarians in ICT.

Resources – virtual classroom

digitalbrain:
http://www.digitalbrain.com/document.server/admin/member.htm

Joint Information Systems Committee's report on VLEs:
http://www.jisc.ac.uk/jtap/htm/jtap-044.html

NOF Training for Teachers:
http://www.nof.org.uk/edu/edu.htm

Large screen displays

There are a number of ways in which you can display the contents of a computer screen on to a large screen. These include connecting your computer to:

- a television;
- an LCD panel;
- a data projector;
- an interactive whiteboard;
- plasma displays.

An LCD panel is placed on top of an overhead projector (OHP). The OHP should be a minimum of 400 W, as the quality of the image relies on the quality of the OHP and on light levels. A data projector is equipment that connects to the computer and projects the image directly onto a screen. Prices range from around £1,200 to over £8,000. The price tends to reflect the resolution, brightness and weight of the equipment.

Interactive whiteboards need to be connected to both a computer and data projector. They tend to be touch sensitive and you can normally operate the computer software from the whiteboard itself by touching the screen, either with a special pen or even with your fingers.

Plasma displays are a relatively new technology that is very expensive. They are large flat monitors which accept both data and video input and provide large screen images. They have the advantages of being able to operate in any light conditions and do not distort the image.

Whatever solution you decide to use, what is important is that the screen is large enough for you to demonstrate or present whatever you are doing on the computer to large groups. A lower-resolution option such as a television screen does not display smaller text and details very effectively, and so detailed material on, for example, a CD ROM may not be readable.

Therefore, it is advisable that you consider an LCD panel, data projector, interactive electronic whiteboard or a plasma screen. These latter solutions do not come cheap. However, the benefits are great. They enable teachers to use the technology in an environment with which they are completely familiar and at home – at the front of the classroom! This is one way in which to encourage teachers to use and practise with the technology, hence improving their IT and ICT skills.

The types of activities you could demonstrate to pupils include:

- word processing;
- spreadsheets/data-handling;
- the Internet;
- CD ROM;
- video;
- any other software you have on the computer.

In addition, you can share with the class an e-mail, a live, online chat or a MUD/MOO session (see Chapter 4, Talk! Talk! Talk!). This enables you, as a teacher, to spread what are often limited resources to benefit more pupils.

Resources – large screen displays

Accurate plc (projectors/interactive whiteboards):
http://www.accurate.plc.uk/

Betterbox (computer to TV adapters/leads):
http://www.betterbox.com/

Boxlight Ltd (plasma displays/projectors):
http://www.boxlight.com/uk

Atomwide Ltd (interactive whiteboards/large screen monitors/projectors):
http://www.atomwide.co.uk/

Bullet Points Presentations Ltd (LCD projectors and panels/interactive whiteboards/large screen monitors):
http://www.bullet-point.co.uk/

eNote Europe.com (LCD panels integrated to laptops):
http://www.webofed.co.uk

Hills Components Ltd (computer to TV adapters/leads):
http://www.hillscomponents.ltd.uk/

Interactive Whiteboard Company:
http://www.iwb.co.uk

Matrix Display Systems (projectors/interactive whiteboards, plasma screens):
http://www.matrixdisplay.com/

Misco Computer Supplies (UK) (computer to TV adapters/LCD panels/leads):
http://www.misco.co.uk/

Promethean (interactive whiteboards/projectors):
http://www.promethean.co.uk

Research Machines (computer to TV adapters/interactive whiteboards/large screen monitors and TVs/LCD projectors):
http://www.rmplc.co.uk/

SMART Board (distributed in the UK by the Steljes Group):
http://www.smartboard.co.uk/

Vupoint (projectors/interactive whiteboards):
http://www.vupoint.co.uk/

Local Grids for Learning

The National Grid for Learning (NGfL) has spawned a number of geographically located 'local' grids, most of which are managed by the local education authorities. Most of these local grids can be accessed via the NGfL under their Community Grid section (http://www.ngfl.gov.uk/comgrids/). A community grid covers more areas of interest than solely education. It can include information on local events, council services, tourism and new developments. If you explore a few of the grids on offer, you will find the results of a variety of interpretations about what a grid should provide.

One of the major difficulties faced by those who provide information electronically, such as on an intranet or a local Grid for Learning, is the issue of how users can search and find content. As we have already mentioned earlier in this chapter, Web site developers are beginning to use databases to store information and that allow individuals to access and display this information via the Web. You might well never know that a site you're visiting is database-driven, since the Web pages appear on your screen just like any other page. However, if you take a look at the source code

```
Source of: wysiwyg://171/http://ferl.becta.org.uk/ - Netscape

<BASE HREF="http://ferl.becta.org.uk/">
```

Figure 3.6 *The source code of the FERL site*

(see Chapter 2, Web authoring), you will notice that there is very little HTML used to produce the page. All the information being displayed via the Web page is hidden away in a database, to which you do not have direct access.

So, for example, the source code of the main Home Page of the FERL site shown in Figure 3.6 results in the image in Figure 3.7 being displayed via a Web browser.

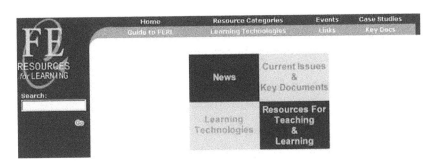

Figure 3.7 *The FERL Web Home Page*

Indexing information and resources

Database-driven sites are easier to update and maintain and are often easier to search, provided that the information is correctly indexed. If the content is not indexed in a consistent manner, it becomes virtually impossible to find all the resources you're looking for, as any librarian can tell you.

Even if the information is not held in a database but within basic Web pages, it still needs to be indexed consistently in order for search tools to find it. The terms used to describe content on a Web page are 'meta-tags' or 'metadata'. Metadata might include the author's name, a title, the language, and keywords to describe the content.

You have just produced a set of Web pages on the war poems of Austin. You could index these pages under any one or combination of keywords: English, poems, war, Austin, Second, World, War, English, writers, and so forth. You could probably think of many more. It would be pretty difficult to find your set of Web pages if you indexed them under 'poets' and 'literature' and someone decided to search for Austin.

What makes the situation even more confusing is when a set of fixed meta-tags are used on one Web site and work well for searches within that site, but fail to function correctly when the content is transferred to another site, which is indexed using different meta-tags. This same issue arises when content from one virtual learning system is imported into another system that uses a different indexing system.

Organizations across the United Kingdom and even Europe are trying to reach agreement on 'standards', that is, on a common indexing system. Not all these standards are yet finalized. However, you can take a look at what standards other large, national learning organizations, such as the University for Industry, are using by checking their site (http://www.ufiltd.co.uk/). Until national standards are agreed, you would be well advised to reach agreement within your own school on an indexing system for your Web and intranet pages.

Resources – metadata and indexing

The Basics of Meta Tags:
http://www.virtualpromote.com/metatag2.html

Metadata Introduction and Discussion Group:
http://ferl.becta.org.uk/features/metadata/metadatamain.htm

Dublin Core Metadata Initiative:
http://purl.oclc.org/dc/

The University for Industry Standards on Learning Content Interworking:
http://www.ufiltd.co.uk/materials/qualified.htm

Other Internet tools of the trade

FTP (file transfer protocol)

FTP has been around about as long as the Internet itself. FTP enables you to log on to a computer and copy files from and to that computer using something called the file transfer protocol, hence the name FTP. To use FTP, it helps if you have *dedicated FTP software* on your machine designed to make the whole process of sending and receiving files easier.

However, some Web browsers such as Netscape, Microsoft Internet Explorer and Fresco let you access FTP servers in the same way you access World Wide Web servers and allow you to receive and send files. In fact, Web browsers make it so easy, you may have already used one to download a file from an FTP site without even knowing it.

The only way to find out if you're connected to an FTP site using a Web browser is to look at the address at the top (the URL). If it's got the word 'ftp' in front of it, you know you've hit the jackpot.

Example:
ftp://ftp.demon.co.uk

However, you may find that dedicated FTP packages are often quicker at fetching and placing files via FTP than using a Web browser. If you think you'll be doing a great deal of file transfer, it would make sense to get yourself a dedicated package.

FTP files can be of any type: text, graphics, audio, video or even software. Most organizations, particularly educational ones, provide an enormous number of files free of charge to the public. All you need is an Internet connection.

In order to gain access to this collection of files, you have to use your dedicated FTP software OR your Web browser to log on to the computer that has the files stored on it, that is, the FTP site. Organizations often require you to have a username, an ID (identification) and a password to gain access to their FTP site but once you have access, you will be able to receive *and* place files at the site.

Luckily, if all you want to do is transfer files one way, from the FTP site to your machine, there are many organizations that will let you log on to the public part of their FTP site as an 'anonymous' user. Basically, you type in your username as 'anonymous'. You will then be prompted for a password.

It is customary on the Internet for 'anonymous' users to enter their e-mail address as their password. After you have been given permission to log on to the remote computer, you can transfer any file you find on the site to your own computer. It's a bit like logging on to a local computer network and downloading files off the server.

For example, imagine you work for a company called 3dftp. You could connect to the public folders on the FTP site of Demon Computers by entering as an anonymous user.

As far as FTP is concerned, Web browsers are easier to use as they automatically log you into the FTP site as an 'anonymous' user and enter your e-mail address as the password. In a Web browser, an FTP directory is presented as a list of links. Clicking on a directory link displays a subdirectory with its directories and files.

If, on the other hand, you have permission to log on and place files on a site, you can use your FTP software or Web browser to also 'upload' (send) files to the site. FTP is still the method most commonly used to transfer completed Web pages to a server (computer) in order for them to be viewed by anyone who has access to that server.

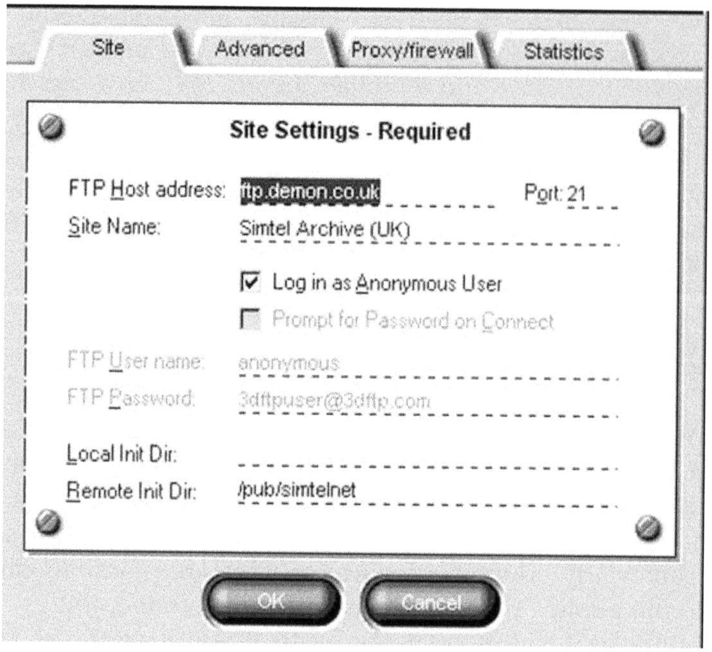

Figure 3.8   *FTP software*

Therefore, the ability to FTP files is an important skill to learn if you hope to set up a school Web site on a server that is *not* located in the school itself.

There are a number of dedicated FTP packages available. One example for each type of machine most commonly found in UK schools is given in the 'Resources – FTP' section below. Search the Web for other examples by using one of the search tools mentioned elsewhere in this chapter.

One further crucial comment on FTP is required. When you access an FTP site you might find that the directory contains a list of folders and files. These will be listed by name, but you will not always have any other explanation as to what the folders might contain or what the files might be, whether they are pictures or sounds or movies! If you're lucky, you might find a document called 'index' or 'readme' which gives you an index of the files on the site, but even these might not prove very helpful. At the moment, there's no foolproof way round this problem.

Resources – FTP

Collection of FTP software (Macintosh):
http://www.macorchard.com/ftp.html

Collection of FTP software (Windows):
http://cws.internet.com/ftp.html

FTPc (Acorn):
http://www.ftpc.iconbar.com/

File formats

On your travels along the Internet route, you will find that many Internet sites make files available for a number of different computers: the IBM-compatible PC, Macintosh, Acorn, Unix etc. Your browser can display some but not all of these formats, so you will probably need to be able to identify file types in order to know whether they will work on your computer. File types also reveal whether you will need additional software to decompress, play or view them.

The way you can identify the format of a file is by looking at its extension, which is usually expressed as a dot followed by two to four letters, the most common being three letters.

All of the file formats found on the Internet can be broken into one of two basic types: ASCII format and BINARY format. ASCII files are text files you can view using any text editor or word processor, whereas binary files contain non-ASCII characters.

If you display a binary file on your screen, you will see a lot of strange symbols and characters that look like utter rubbish. In most cases, if you are not using a Web browser to download the file, you need to set your FTP software to the 'binary' setting to download sounds, images, movies or software. Some up-to-date FTP software can be placed on an 'automatic' setting that will automatically recognize whether the file is ASCII or BINARY.

Table 3.1 *File formats*

Format	Description
.txt	A plain (ASCII) text file. File type: ASCII Requires a word processor or a simple text editor to view them.
.doc	A formatted text file. File type: ASCII Files with this extension are not text documents but are often created using packages like Microsoft Word or WordPerfect for Windows.
.pdf	A Portable Document Format. File type: Binary Requires Adobe Acrobat Reader for the Macintosh and Windows to view them. Acrobat Reader is free and available via the Web. A pdf file is a formatted document that, when viewed, looks the same on every machine.
.ps	A PostScript file. File type: ASCII A PostScript file is unreadable except by a PostScript printer or with the help of an onscreen viewer like Ghostscript, which is available for Macintosh and Windows.
.html/.htm	The language in which Web documents are authored. File type: ASCII. Requires a Web browser to view them.

Graphics formats

At the moment, the graphics formats found on the Web are mainly those with the extension .GIF and .JPEG/.JPG. The great thing about these two formats is that they are platform-independent, which means you can use them on a PC, Macintosh or Acorn (see Chapter 2, Using graphics). Most modern Web browsers can view these formats.

However, you might still come across other image formats on FTP sites, such as .tiff files, in which case you will need external viewers to view the image. Try *Lview Pro for Windows* to view images on a PC, *GIF Converter* for Macintosh users, and *ImageFS* for the Acorn.

All graphics files can be viewed, created or manipulated with graphics software. Try the shareware program *Paint Shop Pro* for the PC, *Graphics Converter* for the Macintosh, or a commercial product such as *Photoshop* available for both Windows and the Macintosh.

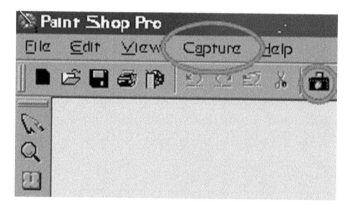

Figure 3.9   *Shareware graphics software: Paint Shop Pro*

Resources – graphics

GIF Converter and image packages (Macintosh):
http://sunsite.org.uk/packages/mac/Collections/sumex/_Graphic_&_Sound_Tool/_Graphic/

Graphics Converter (Macintosh):
http://sunsite.org.uk/packages/mac/Collections/sumex/_Graphic_&_Sound_Tool/_Graphic/

Lview Pro and other image packages (Windows):
http://sunsite.org.uk/packages/ibmpc/collections/simtel/win95/graphics/

Graphics Viewers (Acorn):
http://sunsite.org.uk/packages/archimedes/collections/unistuttgart/riscos/graphics/tools/

Paint Shop Pro (Windows):
http://www.jasc.com/

Adobe Photoshop (Windows and Macintosh):
http://www.adobe.com/

Video formats

For video, the popular extensions are .AVI for the PC, .MPG (MPEG) which is platform-independent but requires its own player, and .MOV and .QT (QuickTime
movies) which were initially for the Macintosh, but are now available for Windows.

.QT, .MOV, .AVI and .MPG files can all be accessed by using QuickTime software,
available for both the Macintosh and Windows. Empire is available for the Acorn.

Resources – video

Quicktime (Windows and Macintosh):
http://www.quicktime.apple.com

Empire (Acorn):
http://www.uniqueway.co.uk/software/empire.html

General Acorn Software:
http://www.riscos.com/

Sound formats

The most popular extensions on the Web for sound are .WAV for the PC, and .AIFF
and .AU for the Macintosh. You can only play these sound files after you've downloaded them to your machine. However, you may well come across streamed audio
and video. Streamed media means that you can hear the sounds and view the video
as soon as they start downloading to your machine rather than have to wait until the
entire file is downloaded. Real Audio and Video, and MP3 technologies, are examples
of streamed media but what's useful is that, if you don't want to hear the music or
watch the video as it slowly downloads, you save the MP3 and Real Audio/Video files
to your machine first and then access them locally.

Both Windows and Macintosh computers can use QuickTime to play .AU and .AIFF
files, whilst WHAM (Waveform – Hold and Modify) can be used on Windows systems.

.RA and MP3 files can be played using the Real Audio Player, either for the
Macintosh or Windows. You can also use QuickTime to play MP3 files.

Acorn machines could use SoundCon for most sound files and AMP Radio for
streamed MP3 files.

Resources – sound

QuickTime (Windows and Macintosh):
http://www.quicktime.apple.com

Real Player (Windows and Macintosh):
http://www.real.co.uk/

MP3 software (Windows and Macintosh):
http://software.mp3.com/software/

Sound players (Windows):
http://www.supernet.net/cwsapps/

WHAM (Windows):
http://www.supernet.net/cwsapps/ssound.html

AMP Radio (Macintosh):
http://www.subband.com/ampr/download.html

Sound players (Acorn):
http://www.acornusers.org/cbsa/Audio.html

Squeezing it all in

If you intend to make extensive use of the resources you find on the Internet, you're going to have to learn about encoding and compression formats. As mentioned in Chapter 4, So how do you do it?, when files are sent via e-mail they are encoded. If your e-mail package does not deal with all the encoding formats, you will need separate software that can decode these files depending on which format was used to encode them in the first place.

But decoding the file is not always the end of the story. Files available on UseNet newsgroups, FTP sites and bulletin boards are very likely to be compressed so as to take up less space on the server's hard disk.

Most of the files you encounter on the Web will either be text, graphics, audio or video files. Some may be compressed, others will not. The most common compressed files you will encounter are those with extensions such as .ZIP, .HQX or .ARC. These extensions represent the most commonly used compression formats for the PC, Macintosh and Acorn. Sometimes, you may encounter files with multiple extensions, which usually means that more than one type of software was used to compile and compress the file.

Example:
louvre.*zip* (is compressed using the PKZIP format used by PCs)

Sites that deal with Acorn/Archimedes software compress using software called Spark. SparkPlug is available to decompress these files. IBM-compatible machines use predominantly PKZIP, whilst Macintosh machines use Binhex. But you're likely to come across a few other compression formats (.tar, .gzip) which are Unix-based since many servers that form part of the Internet are still Unix machines.

Figure 3.10 summarizes the main compression and encoding formats and examples of the relevant software you will need to decompress them, depending on whether you're using an IBM, Macintosh or Acorn machine.

Format	Compression/decompression software		
Extension	IBM-compatible	Macintosh	Acorn/Archimedes
.zip Zip is the standard on the MS-DOS machines	For Windows: WinZip or Stuffit Expander for Windows	Zipit (Shareware)	!SparkFS
.arc	Stuffit Expander for Windows	Stuffit Expander for the Mac (works in conjunction with the program Stuffit Lite, DropStuff with Expander Enhancer, or Stuffit Deluxe)	!SparkPlug
.sit .bin .hqx (most common Mac archiving and compression programs)	Stuffit Expander for Windows	Stuffit Expander for the Mac extracts Stuffit archives but does not create them – freeware)	!SparkFS

Figure 3.10 *Common compression formats*

Resources – compression and decompression tools

PKZip (Windows):
http://www.interpages.co.uk/pkzipage/

WinZip (Windows):
http://www.winzip.com/

Stuffit Expander (Windows and Macintosh):
http://www.aladdinsys.com/

Sparkplug and SparkFS (Acorn):
http://www.netlink.co.uk/users/pilling/

4

Communicating and learning via the Net

So far, we have talked about the Internet predominantly as a source of information, a place to go and find, retrieve and save valuable resources or as a place where you can publish your own school site. Although these are both important functions of the Internet, particularly the Web, it can play other roles too! Further useful functions include:

- supporting collaborative working practices;
- allowing staff and pupils to share resources.

Chapter 2 has already provided some information on the use of the Web as a publicity and publication medium for schools. The next section will concentrate on collaborative working and then examine a range of other Internet tools. It is important here to remind readers that this book is not for beginners, but is intended for users who already have some experience of the Internet and the Web.

Collaborative working

Collaboration is a form of communication, but one that is often focused on a specific aim and is time-limited. It is a way of people networking and working together on a particular task or project.

Electronic communications technologies are a powerful way of enabling collaborative working at a distance. They can bring together individuals from different organizations in different locations and provide them with the tools to work together as a group.

Electronic networks have the advantage of making available new information almost instantaneously. Transmitting information in a digital form allows individuals and groups to find, send, receive and store large amounts of data.

However, collaborative working does not just happen because you have a number of people each with electronic access to one another. By taking time to assess current or planned collaborative working, you might save yourself and your school some major headaches in the future. Before plunging into online collaboration, it might be worth a few minutes to ask yourself and your school managers a few of the following questions.

Online or not online?

1. Would the cost of travel put attendance of meetings beyond the means of all or some of the participants?
2. Are there deadlines that electronic collaboration could help you meet quicker and more easily?
3. Is there one participant willing to act as a facilitator? Would the facilitator be willing to spend the time to manage the collaborative process electronically?
4. Is the technology easily accessible to all the participants? Can collaboration occur effectively with only a few key participants working online?
5. Will training for participants be required? How long will this take and how much will it cost?
6. Who will provide technical assistance?
7. Can the nature of the discussions and collaborative process be captured electronically and archived?
8. Will the technology be mainly text-orientated, and if so, will this communication medium be a barrier for some participants? Can this barrier be overcome?

Collaborative working of any type is more successful if one member of the team is designated as the facilitator. Online collaboration requires not only the presence of a facilitator, but the added requirement that all participants make use of their online facilities regularly. So if e-mail is the method of communication selected, participants should check their e-mail often and respond to those messages requiring action.

The more widely spread the participants geographically, the less opportunity there is for face-to-face meetings and the more important the role electronic networking could play. Information and communications technologies are often successful in supporting already existing relationships between individuals, groups and organizations but they can also encourage otherwise disparate strangers to communicate and share information.

So how do you do it?

There are a number of tools you can use to collaborate online and these are all either synchronous or asynchronous methods of communication. Synchronous (real-time) communication includes tools that require all the users to be online at the same time to take part in discussions. Asynchronous (not real-time) communication is where users do not need to be online simultaneously to communicate.

The most well-known asynchronous software is our good friend the electronic mail (e-mail) system. Although never really developed as a conferencing tool, an e-mail package such as Microsoft Outlook or Pegasus will make an adequate start, particularly if you use it to join a mailing list (see below). Equally, browsers like Netscape Communicator offer e-mail as part of their facilities.

Another method is the use of a dedicated group conferencing package such as FirstClass or WebBoard. A dedicated system usually contains both asynchronous and synchronous features necessary to support online conferencing such as e-mail, the ability to archive messages into separate folders, bulletin boards, file sharing, and real-time text-based chat. In addition, you can also use Web conferencing tools which can be accessed via the Web itself.

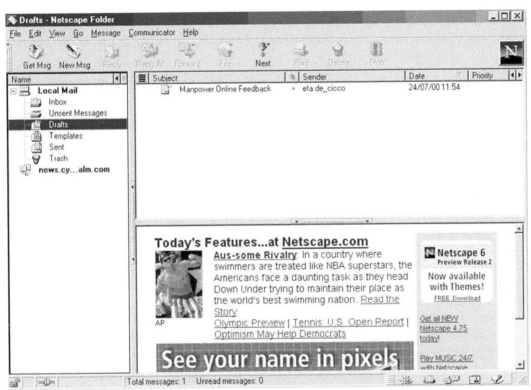

Figure 4.1 *Netscape's e-mail facility*

Finally, you could use what is called 'groupware', a class of software that provides a variety of functions that facilitate individuals working together. These systems include features that support communications, collaboration and coordination. One example of groupware is Lotus Notes.

You may decide to opt for one of these choices, or for a combination. But first, let's take a look at each of these options separately, starting with the simplest tool – electronic mail.

Electronic mail

Internet electronic mail (e-mail) is a way of sending a message to either an individual or to a group of individuals. Much like sending a letter via the postal services to a specific address, you can send e-mail to anyone on the Internet who has an Internet e-mail address. You don't need to be using the same Internet service provider as the recipient.

The speed of delivery is one important benefit of e-mail, but there are others. Using e-mail offers you the opportunity to overcome the limitations of time, and can be more economical than equivalent alternatives. Basically, you can communicate with others in different countries, even those in different time zones, for the cost of a local telephone call and the subscription charges of your Internet service provider. You send messages when it is convenient for you and the recipients can pick them up when it's convenient for them.

In addition, it is possible to send one or more messages to a group of people in one single operation. Most modern e-mail packages have the facility that enables you to create your own group addresses. Each group contains the e-mail addresses of selected individuals, and you can often add and remove names from the group. This makes it much easier and quicker to communicate with a large number of people.

The downside to e-mail communication is that it cannot guarantee privacy. Internet e-mail can be read by *any* system administrator of any of the computers that handle the message on its way to your desktop. Although it's unlikely that someone will pick your message out of the thousands of e-mails that flow through computers, you can never be absolutely sure. So unless you are using reliable encryption software, never write anything in an e-mail you wouldn't mind being broadcast to the world.

Equally, do not assume that your e-mail has been delivered to its destination, or that it has been read. E-mail may fail to be delivered for any number of reasons: the recipient's computer dealing with e-mail (the e-mail server) may be down, you may encounter broken connections along the way, or you might have made an error when typing in the e-mail address. Even should it arrive on the recipient's desktop, never assume it has been read. Unless you know that the individual you are e-mailing reads his or her e-mail regularly, always allow for the fact that not everyone has either instant or constant e-mail access.

Tips for making best use of e-mail:

- E-mail should be checked regularly – at least once a week, daily if possible.
- E-mail messages should be kept short. Long messages are harder to read on a computer screen. If the document is a long one, and your e-mail package has the facility, send the document as an enclosure/attachment.
- E-mail is more suited to informal communication and is highly conversational.
- Try to stick to one single issue in each e-mail message, otherwise people will tend to get confused between the different threads of conversation.
- E-mail depends mainly on text to convey meaning. Emotion and tone of voice are lost. There are conventions that attempt to overcome this handicap. Try to familiarize yourself with them.
- Keep copies of any important messages you send for your own reference or in case they fail to arrive safely and you need to resend it.
- E-mail is never completely secure, although encryption software can help.

Finally, modern e-mail packages give you the facility to send attachments or enclosures with your message. These can be any types of file – a text document, a piece of software, a sound or picture file, or even a movie. However, there are some factors you have to take into consideration when sending files via e-mail.

You will find that attaching files means they will be encoded, as this is the only way e-mail can deliver different types of files electronically. There are different e-mail encoding standards, or protocols, and these depend on what type of computer the sender and recipient are using.

With the more recent e-mail packages, an e-mail message will state, as part of its message, what type of encoding has occurred and, on the whole, you shouldn't encounter too many difficulties reading attachments. Otherwise, you may well need additional software on your machine that can decode the attachments (see Chapter 3, Squeezing it all in).

You may find that certain Internet service providers set a maximum file size limit on both the size of the message and the size of any enclosures. Certain files, particularly pictures and movies, can be very large and have to be compressed in order to make them smaller, easier and quicker to transmit. Again, you need separate software on your computer that can both compress and uncompress files. If the file is still too big, even when compressed, and the recipient has access to file transfer protocol (FTP), FTP it to him or her.

Alternatively, you could use a Web-based facility that allows you to send and store large files on its server, therefore allowing other individuals to download the file from any computer with an Internet connection. FilePool is such an example. It's important that when you use these types of facilities, you note the address of the Web page allocated to the file you are storing. Without it, you won't be able to trace the file.

Finally, you need to make sure that those receiving your attachments have either the same make of software you used to create the file, or another package that can handle that type of file. For example, if you used Microsoft Word to create the text file you e-mailed over, the recipient will usually either need to have the same version or a more recent version of Microsoft Word *or* another package that can read Word files. If you used Microsoft Excel to produce a spreadsheet, the recipient will either need the same or a more recent version of Microsoft Excel *or* another package that can deal with Excel files to look at the spreadsheet.

Well, that's the complicated bit out of the way. Now let's briefly mention e-mail rules. Yes, there are such things and they have developed over time to make e-mail messages easier to use and understand. They are quite simple but very effective. Symbols have slowly developed called 'emoticons' or 'smiley faces', which are intended to represent a human face. These smileys represent various human facial expressions such as a smile or frown.

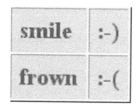

Figure 4.2 *Two most commonly used smileys*

Because e-mail correspondence tends to be asynchronous, where the recipients might read your message days or even weeks after you've sent it, you need to provide a context in which to read the message. So what do we mean by context? Let's compare the three examples below.

Example I:
Sounds fine by me.

This e-mail really tells the recipient very little. Your reply might be a response to one of hundreds of messages they have e-mailed out. Unless they remember exactly what you are agreeing with, it would take them some time to trace their previous e-mail to you and reread it. It would be much better if you provided some context for your reply:

Example II:
> so I was thinking we might meet up Friday 22nd at 2.00 pm
Sounds fine by me.

The '>' is one of the conventions for quoting someone else's words. It refers people to the relevant parts of their message to you and is immediately followed by your reply. You should include just enough content to provide a context for the reply and no more. You can even quote back two or three different parts of someone else's message, each with a separate reply.

Example III:
> Have you talked to the English Department about those CD ROMs we discussed at the
> staff meeting?
Yes. They were keen to go ahead and order them. I'll let you have the budget code when I next see you.
> I thought the document you sent me was very interesting, particularly the section on
> integrating videoconferencing in classroom practice.
Agreed. I think we ought to set up a presentation and demo of the system at the next staff training day.

As you can see, by providing context for your replies, the e-mail not only makes more sense, it is easier to read and assimilate. And your recipient will thank you for it.

Resources – e-mail

Eudora for Macintosh:
ftp.eudora.com

Pegasus (Windows):
http://www.pegasus.usa.com/

Microsoft Outlook Express (Windows):
http://www.microsoft.com/

TTFN (The Thread Following Newsreader) (Acorn):
http://www.arcade.demon.co.uk/ttfn.html

Mailing lists

Mailing lists (also known as e-mail lists) sprang up from the need to exploit e-mail's ability to post electronic messages to a group of people. Those who participate in a mailing list often share a common interest. A participant sends a message to one e-mail address only, and that message is then redistributed to every mailing list member. The mailing list can be either fully automated (maintained by a computer) or operated by a person (who might manually collect and redistribute the messages). In addition, a mailing list can be set up to be open to all members of the public or a closed group, in which only specific individuals can join.

The advantages of mailing lists over traditional methods such as mail merges and long-distance faxes is the considerable reduction in costs, the speed of delivery and the fact that material arrives in a digital format and can therefore be easily customized. By participating in a mailing list, people who share a common interest can engage in discussion or seek advice and help from other participants. Mailing lists and newsgroups (see below) are a very good source of expertise on particular topics and can often help participants solve particular problems.

One important fact to remember is that e-mail still depends mainly on text to convey meaning. It's very easy to offend individuals accidentally by, for example, writing what you intend to be a funny, joking comment but which is received as criticism. As in all types of text-based communication methods, conventions have developed that attempt to overcome this handicap. Try to familiarize yourself with them if you don't want to get *flamed*. Getting flamed means you receive either harsh, inflammatory responses or actual personal attacks via e-mail.

The benefits of mailing lists and newsgroups are the ability to engage in discussion of specific issues, tap into expertise and experience, and share information. The downside is that subscribing to mailing lists can generate many messages, often swamping your e-mail account.

Common features of mailing lists:

- You can receive individual messages from the list daily or choose to receive a regular, often weekly or fortnightly, digest that consolidates all e-mails into one full-text message.
- You can suspend messages temporarily in case you're out of school for a while or on holiday, and then re-establish membership on your return.
- You can unsubscribe from the list at any time.

If you're finding that you're receiving far too many messages from a mailing list but you don't want to unsubscribe from it, you might find that your e-mail package enables you to filter messages, so that certain e-mails are either deleted automatically or filed in a separate folder. If you don't have this facility, check whether the mailing list has a *digest* version. A digest collects all the messages together over a given period of time and often organizes them by topic with an index.

Some mailing list services, such as JISCmail, offer the facility for lists to store their message archives on the Web where you can view them using your Web browser. An archive stores all the messages the mailing list has sent and received and is a useful tool for browsing past information. It is worth taking a look at a list's archives before deciding whether it will be of relevance to you.

Resources – mailing lists

Comprehensive lists of e-mail discussion groups:
http://www.liszt.com
http://www.jiscmail.ac.uk
http://catalog.com/vivian/interest-group-search.html

National Grid for Learning's Virtual Teacher Centre discussion groups:
http://vtc.ngfl.gov.uk

JISCmail discussion lists:
http://www.jiscmail.ac.uk

uk-schools
http://www.jiscmail.ac.uk/lists/uk-schools.html
A list for teachers and others interested in the use of the Internet in UK schools and for general discussion about anything concerning international classroom connections.

basic-skills
http://www.jiscmail.ac.uk/lists/basic-skills.html
This list is intended to provide a forum for discussions relating to the provision and delivery of Basic Skills services, particularly relating to the introduction and use of online and other ICT resources.

ict
http://www.jiscmail.ac.uk/lists/ict.html
A list for announcements and discussion related to the use of information and communication technologies (ICT) and/or information and learning technologies (ILT) in teaching and learning.

ict-support
http://www.jiscmail.ac.uk/lists/ict-support.html
A list to provide peer and expert ICT support for student teachers.

school-management
http://www.jiscmail.ac.uk/lists/school-management.html
A list for discussion of education in schools, in particular their management and government and the curriculum.

teacher-education
http://www.jiscmail.ac.uk/lists/teacher-education.html
Discussion of all aspects of professional education and development for teachers in initial teacher training.

FilePool
http://www.filepool.com/

Web-based e-mail

As the Web grows, Web technology is being used more and more to supplement and sometimes replace other types of technologies. E-mail is still one of the most popular Internet features and a number of Web sites have been developed that offer Web-based e-mail facilities.

Web-based e-mail services allow you to send and receive messages from any computer connected to the Internet. You can use Web-based e-mail systems from home, school, an Internet Cybercafé, or a friend's house. The facility is extremely useful for those people who use more than one computer either because they travel frequently or don't own their own computer. Your messages are stored in a central location and you simply use the Web to access your account.

Hotmail was one of the first Web-based e-mail providers. Now there are many to choose from, such as *Postmaster* and *Talk21*. When you create Web-based accounts, you choose one or more permanent e-mail addresses and these will never change as long as you continue to use them regularly. You can only access your accounts if you have your user identifications and passwords. A major advantage is that most of the Web-based e-mail services are free because they place banner advertising on some of their pages.

The services offered by these sites have improved a great deal over the past few years. They now offer the most common e-mail facilities that have always been available when using 'dedicated' e-mail software, such as:

● your own address book – so you can collect individual e-mails of people you e-mail regularly;
● attachments – so you can add and receive files enclosed with your messages.

However, the major disadvantages are that, for most of the services, you have to be online to compose or reply to your messages, the service can be slow so that there is

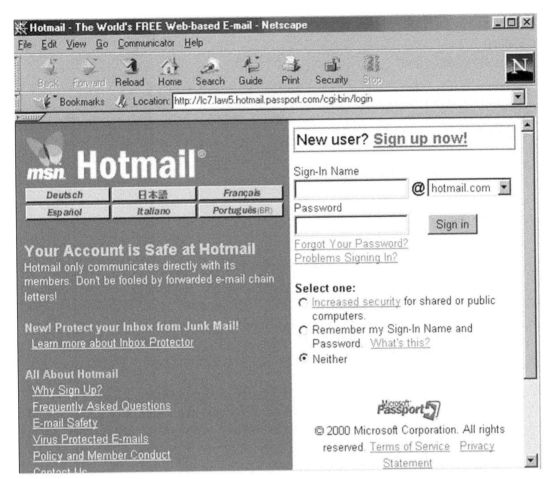

Figure 4.3 *Hotmail's Web-based e-mail facilities*

considerable delay in downloading pages, and finally, each user is limited in the amount of space allocated to them for their e-mails. Hotmail, for example, offers only 2 Mb which can quickly become consumed by hundreds of e-mail messages, both e-mails received and those sent.

eGroups by Yahoo and Coollists are Web-based e-mail services that allow you easily to create your own and join other people's e-mail groups. These services offer the same facilities as many of the non-Web-based mailing lists mentioned above but egroups also includes additional features such as the ability to schedule events using an online calendar and real-time chat (see below).

Not only can you access your e-mail from any Internet-enabled computer in the world, but services are starting to appear that enable you to provide Web-based e-mail on your own Web site so that schools can offer their visitors Web-based e-mail facilities. everyone.net is an example.

Resources – Web-based e-mail

Coollist:
http://www.coollist.com/

Hotmail:
http://www.hotmail.com

Postmaster:
http://www.postmaster.co.uk/

Talk21:
http://www.talk21.com/

e-groups:
http://www.egroups.com/

everyone.net:
http://www.everyone.net/main/html/email_tour.html

Conferencing software

If you would like more versatility when engaged in electronic collaboration, you might want to experiment with dedicated conferencing packages such as First Class. These give you many more functions than e-mail but are often *closed* systems, that is, they can only communicate with individuals who have the same conferencing software and/or who have permission to use the computer where the conferencing discussions and information are kept. Passwords are used to keep intruders out.

Within a conferencing system, for example, you can set up numerous discussion topics, each with its own area for messages and basically acting like giant bulletin boards. First you go online and download the most recent messages in the topic areas that interest you. Then you prepare your replies offline and when you're ready, go back online and place your messages in the topic areas for others to pick up and read later. Easy really! Messages and comments can be archived, allowing you to see how a discussion on a particular topic has progressed, or maybe you want to start an entirely new topic. It's up to you!

Conferencing packages also offer e-mail facilities, but usually only to those who have permission to use the system. Like Internet e-mail, you can attach files to your messages, but unlike Internet e-mail, you'll find that the recipient can open the attached files easily without bothering with decoding or decompressing them. That's because they're using the same software as you are.

Since dedicated conferencing packages are produced to encourage collaboration and communication, they tend to contain scheduling facilities to arrange meetings,

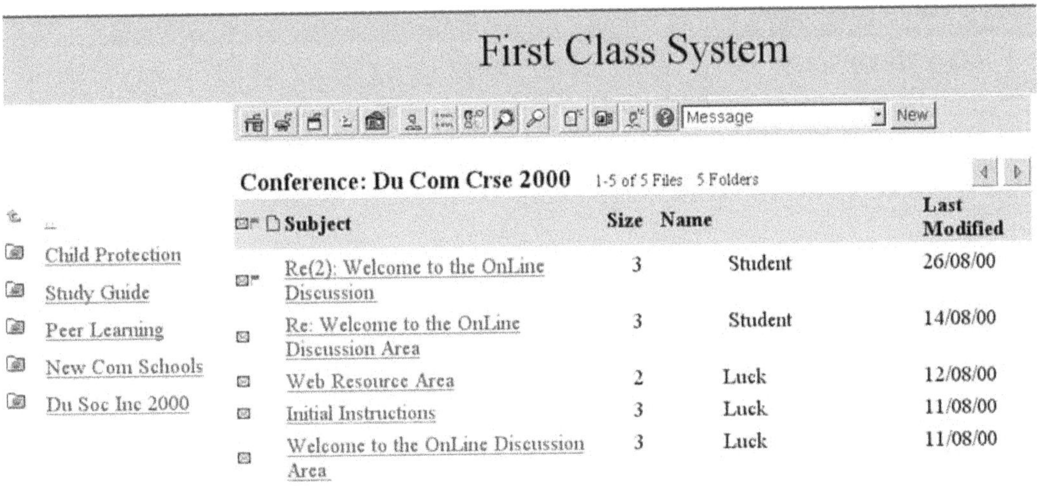

First Class System

Conference: Du Com Crse 2000   1-5 of 5 Files 5 Folders

Subject	Size	Name	Last Modified
Re(2): Welcome to the OnLine Discussion	3	Student	26/08/00
Re: Welcome to the OnLine Discussion Area	3	Student	14/08/00
Web Resource Area	2	Luck	12/08/00
Initial Instructions	3	Luck	11/08/00
Welcome to the OnLine Discussion Area	3	Luck	11/08/00

Child Protection
Study Guide
Peer Learning
New Com Schools
Du Soc Inc 2000

Figure 4.4   *The First Class Conferencing System*

real-time chat (see Talk! Talk! Talk! on p 88), collaborative document editing, search facilities that can find any information stored within files or messages, and the opportunity for you to view details about other users who are on the same system as yourself. You can look at another user's biography, his or her e-mail address, and sometimes even his or her photograph.

Even more impressive, Web-based conferencing software such as WebBoard provides the added benefit of the Web's multimedia environment to the discussion process. Web conferencing software acts like a dedicated conferencing system in that topics can be arranged in logical order, user details can be provided (with the added bonus – or is that embarrassment? of photos, video or sound clips), and past discussions can be archived. In addition, your messages can contain hyperlinks (just like you get on a Web page) or graphics.

Another very basic collaborative tool is NetMeeting, which comprises video, audio and a whiteboard facility (a shared work area). It is already provided with the Microsoft browser Internet Explorer, and is *free* to educational users. NetMeeting works using both the Internet and ISDN (Integrated Services Digital Network). In addition, the software can be used over an internal computer network. Naturally, the faster the speed of your connection, the better the sound and picture quality.

Resources – conferencing software

NetMeeting (Windows):
http://www.microsoft.com/windows/netmeeting/download/nm301x86.asp

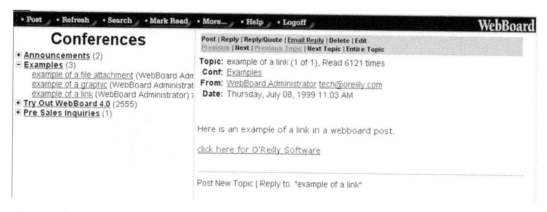

Figure 4.5 *WebBoard Conferencing System*

WebBoard (Windows and Macintosh):
http://webboard.oreilly.com/

FirstClass (Macintosh and Windows):
http://www.softarc.com/

Groupware

Groupware is technology designed to facilitate the work of groups. This technology may be used to communicate, cooperate, coordinate, negotiate, and solve problems. Features of groupware include scheduling, information sharing, e-mail, video, audio, chat and shared whiteboards (a system that allows two or more people to view and draw on an electronic shared workspace). All these aspects work together seamlessly. The advantage of using groupware is a bit like using a word processor, spreadsheet and database, all produced by separate manufacturers and unable to share data, as compared to using an integrated system that combines all three and can exchange information between them.

Resources – groupware

Groupware Central:
http://www.terry.uga.edu/groupware/groupware.html

Usability First site:
http://www.usabilityfirst.com/intro/newcomers.html

Lotus:
http://www.lotus.com/home.nsf/welcome/notesua

Web4:
http://www.jdhtech.com/

Video conferencing

Video conferencing is a form of electronic communication that enables two or more individuals to talk to each other whilst also being able to see each other. Many video conferencing systems connect two sites together; it is possible to have conferences between three or more sites but this requires additional hardware and software.

The majority of video conferencing systems can only operate using ISDN or over local networks, but a number have been developed that function over the Internet, such as CUSeeMe and Dwyco Video Conferencing. Unfortunately, the quality of Internet video conferencing systems cannot as yet compare with systems that use other methods of connectivity.

Unless you have equipment capable of projecting the video image from your video conferencing system onto a large screen, most Internet video conferencing systems are best suited to groups where the number of learners consists of fewer than five individuals. Video conferences can support collaborative working by enabling:

- your school to provide classes to pupils at other schools in shortage subjects;
- your school to offer subjects outside normal school hours;
- pupils to work collaboratively with others on joint assignments;
- pupils to observe and learn specialist skills;
- pupils to practise speaking foreign languages with native speakers;
- schools to communicate with 'video' pals from diverse cultures;
- schools to work with businesses and other partners to enhance the curriculum.

Resources – video conferencing

CUseeMe (Windows and Macintosh):
http://www.cuseeme.com/

Dwyco Video conferencing (Windows):
http://www.dwyco.com/

You can find out more about how Internet video conferencing is being used in schools at:

http://gsh.lightspan.com/cu/index.asp

Internet telephony

Over the past couple of years, Internet technology has developed in such a way that you can now make use of the Internet to make national and international telephone calls. A number of services are available. Many of them require you to download dedicated software to your machine, but one service that does not need additional software is HotTelephone.

However, because these services tend to offer international calls that only cost you the cost of connection to your local Internet provider, and in some cases a very low rate per call, they are extremely popular. HotTelephone's Web site is often busy and unobtainable and in addition, the 'free' registration form asks a fair number of fairly personal questions regarding your finances.

Still, it might be worth checking them out since they are cheaper than using regular telecommunication companies and might come in handy as a backup to e-mail when collaborating with schools abroad.

Resources – Internet telephony

List of Internet telephony resources:
http://www.computertelephony.org/

HotTelephone:
http;//www.hottelephone.com

Net2Phone:
http://www.net2phone.com

Electronic networks

Electronic networking can be put to a couple of other important uses. You can transfer data, such as examination results, payroll information or statistical data, from one location to another, thus saving time and effort. Some colleges of further education are already sending statistical information to their funding councils electronically and school examination details are being transferred to and from Local Education Authorities. In addition, using the technology can result in staff gaining or improving their research, graphic arts and communication skills, thereby contributing to their overall computer literacy.

Talk! Talk! Talk!

Collaborative working is all very well, but there are times when we would like to communicate with like-minded individuals without necessarily working with them on a project or topic. In cases like these, bulletin boards, UseNet newsgroups, Chat, MUDs (multi-user domains) and MOOs (MUD object-oriented) facilities might be useful.

Bulletin boards

Electronic bulletin boards are much like non-electronic public notice boards but instead of pinning up messages on a notice board, you post electronic messages to a bulletin board which is then publicly visible to anyone who has access to it. Bulletin boards need not be available on the Internet; in fact, many of them are not and you have to dial into them. All you need is appropriate *software* to access the bulletin board, a modem and a phone line.

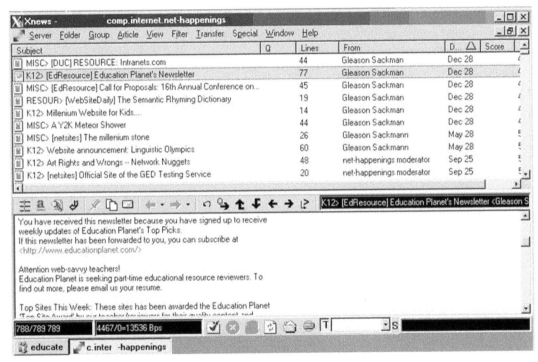

Figure 4.6 *Example of a UseNet newsgroup*

You will find that the majority of bulletin boards are free to join whilst others will require you to pay a subscription fee. Not only do they hold messages, they are a great source of public domain (freeware or shareware) programs and information which can be either of a general or specialist nature. Files held on a bulletin board are often compressed so you'll need to know about the different compression formats (see Chapter 3, Squeezing it all in) to take full advantage of them.

Unfortunately, certain bulletin boards can also hold many files that are considered to be 'unsuitable' for pupils. Often these bulletin boards require a subscription and declaration of age before entry is permitted; however, pupil access to bulletin boards should still be approached with the same awareness as when dealing with any other public electronic network – with caution and care.

Finally, you can learn how to set up a bulletin board on a third party's computer or on your own school server by checking out Web sites listed under Resources – bulletin boards, below.

Resources – bulletin boards

Sample bulletin boards:
http://www.bulletinboards.com/bulletin-board.cfm

Free bulletin board software:
http://www.intrasmart.com/bulletinboardsoftware-hotb.htm
http://www.thedirectory.org/diamond/usoft.htm

UseNet

Bulletin boards vary in size, with some holding fewer than a dozen discussion topics, others many hundreds. UseNet requires either software known as a newsreader to access a server (computer) that carries UseNet groups, or you can set up Microsoft Outlook e-mail software to read UseNet messages.

When you first take a look at UseNet, you could be faced with thousands of topics known as newsgroups. These newsgroups cover discussions on subjects as varied as television soaps, dyslexia, cookery, computer operating systems and much, much more. Newsgroups can be an excellent source of expertise and information. Equally, they can be source of gossip, misinformation and downright dribble!

When you first join a mailing list or access a newsgroup, it would be wise to look at its FAQ (Frequently Asked Questions). The FAQ file might be included in the 'Welcome' message you receive when you first subscribe or available by request from the mailing list. This FAQ file contains all the questions a new entrant (newbie) is likely to ask about the mailing list or newsgroup.

Do try to read it first as nothing irritates other regular users more than a newbie asking basic questions about the list or group that are contained in the FAQ. Once you've read the FAQ, lurk for awhile. Lurking is when you just read messages for a time without replying to them. It's a good way to get to know whether the group you've joined meets your needs and ensures you don't post messages that are inappropriate to the group. Once you've read the appropriate FAQ, you select which newsgroups you want to receive and can then both read postings to those newsgroups and reply to them using the same news server.

Every so often, the server that holds your postings will contact another server that carries UseNet and they each exchange new messages for that day. This type of daily exchange between computers that handle UseNet is repeated around the world, likening UseNet to a globally distributed bulletin board.

When using UseNet, you need to remember that, because new messages are being sent from computer to computer across the globe, two people at different locations in the world might be viewing the same newsgroup at the same time, with each seeing slightly different content. Newer material will appear first on machines nearest to the server where it originated, gradually spreading out across the network.

Depending on the newsgroup, old messages might be kept for a few days or maybe for a month or so, but rarely longer. The amount of traffic generated across the 50,000 plus newsgroups is such that there is rarely enough disk space on servers to keep messages for much longer. It is for this reason that many UseNet providers do not carry all the newsgroups.

Where education is concerned, this might not be a bad thing since there are some newsgroups that would be totally unsuitable for pupils. If you find that your Internet provider offers a UseNet service, it might be worth asking if they could arrange for certain 'undesirable' newsgroups to be filtered out and not made available to your school.

On a positive note, there are a number of newsgroups that are of educational value. These carry not only messages of interest to teachers and pupils but files, which are not solely text, but can be graphics, software or sound. As with e-mail, you have to learn about encoding and compression formats to view them.

If all that sounds complicated, don't panic! There are several utilities or even news-readers available that will automatically paste together the many parts of an encoded file for you so it can be decoded.

Finally, if you are short of time but would like to view the most recent discussions about a particular topic, just use a *search engine* that searches UseNet postings. One particularly good search engine that only deals with newsgroups can be found on the Web at:

http://www.deja.com

Resources – UseNet

List of newsreaders (Windows):
http://cws.internet.com/news.html

NewsWatcher (Macintosh):
http://sunsite.doc.ic.ac.uk/packages/info-mac/comm/_Internet/

Messenger Pro newsreader (Acorn):
http://www.rcomp.co.uk/

List of public newsgroups in the UK:
http://www.usenet.org.uk/newsgroups.html

List of global newsgroups:
http://www.liszt.com/news/

Internet Relay Chat (IRC)

Until the emergence of the Web, communication on the Internet was conducted predominantly via a text interface. And despite the use of multimedia to smarten up Web pages, one of the most popular uses of the Internet remains e-mail.

Internet Relay Chat is a form of online, real-time discussion using text as the main form of communication. Once you have the right piece of Internet Relay Chat software on your machine, you can link up with other individuals who have the software running by directing your software towards an IRC server (machine). It's a cross between a bulletin board and e-mail.

Topics and themes are referred to as chat rooms or channels. When you join a discussion about a theme or topic, you adopt an identity that you want to use during the chat. This identity could be based on true characteristics about yourself, or on a fictitious character. Then, any contributions you make to the chat appear on the screen alongside the comments of other contributors who are logged on to the chat channel at the same time.

At the start, IRC forums might appear somewhat confusing, with different comments appearing next to one another in no particular order, but you soon get used to the style. IRC is definitely not for novices so read the 'Help' file first before diving in. As with everything, practice is the key.

Since chat is predominantly text-based, a certain style of language and use of acronyms has developed that requires persistence to master. Grammar and spelling norms are not necessarily adhered to within e-mail, bulletin boards and particularly in chat. It is not uncommon to find whole paragraphs typed in lower case, and containing more than one typo or spelling error. In addition, acronyms have been developed to try to overcome the inadequacies of the written word in conveying emotion and body language. An example of this would be the use of BTW to mean *by the way* or LOL to mean *laughing out loud*.

Since chat still tends to be dominated by trivial topics and can contain undesirable subjects of discussion, you are advised to guarantee supervision if you intend to enable pupils to learn the technology using general chat sites. In the past few years, chat facilities have become available via the Web and there are specific Web chat facilities, such as *FreeZone for Kids* and *Kids Chat*, which are aimed directly at children. These sites are moderated in order to ensure the safety of its young users.

Resources – Internet Relay Chat

mIRC (Windows):
http://www.mirc.co.uk/

M_ircle (Macintosh):
http://www.ircle.com/

IRC (Acorn):
http://www.acornusers.org/cbsa/Internet.html

Freezone for Kids (all school age groups):
http://chat.freezone.com/

Kids Chat (for young children):
http://www.sutton.lincs.sch.uk/kidstest/start.htm

Anexa (create your own chat areas):
http://www.anexa.com/

EduCentre (American site for chats on educational issues):
http://home.talkcity.com/LibraryDr/edupeople/

Instant messaging software

Instant messaging software comprises tools that, once installed, inform you when individuals are online, therefore allowing you to communicate with them. Software in this category include ICQ, Infoseek Instant Messaging and MSN Messenger Service. Some of these tools also allow you to telephone or page individuals via the Net, share files, play games, or just chat, using text, with other people online.

Resources – instant messaging software

ICQ:
http://www.mirabilis.com/

Infoseek Instant Messaging:
http://www.peoplelink.com/v1/down_infoseek/

MSN Messenger Service:
http://messenger.msn.com/

MOOs and MUDs

MOO is simply a form of text-based virtual reality that users can access and interact with over the Internet. MOO stands for MUD object oriented, where MUD stands for multi-user domain.

Both MOOs and MUDs are software programs that accept 'connections' from multiple users across a network and provide each user access to a shared database. Participants have the appearance of being situated in an artificially constructed place (a room) that also contains other players who are connected at the same time.

A MUD user's interface to the database is text-based and users communicate in real time, that is, you have to type in sentences to communicate with others. Unlike adventure games online, a MUD is not goal-oriented. It has no beginning, end or 'winning scores'.

Users with the right permissions can add new objects to the database such as more rooms, notes to read or other 'things'. Generally, MUDs and MOOs have more than one user connected at a time. All of the connected users are manipulating the same database (and therefore objects) and can encounter any newly formed object created by others. MUD players spend most of their connected time socializing with each other, exploring the various rooms and objects and adding new objects of their own design.

You access MOOs and MUDs either via the Web or by using dedicated software. Like a browser, dedicated software has to have an address of a computer in order to connect with it. This address is referred to as the *host* computer. You might also have to provide a *port* number to tell the computer where the MUD/MOO environment is located.

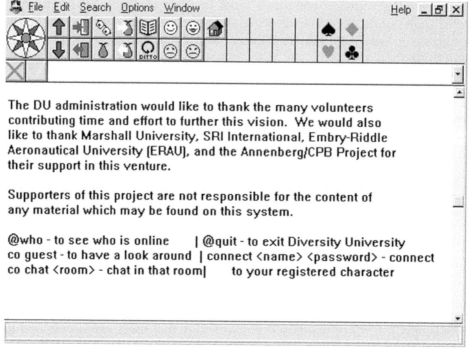

Figure 4.7 *Typical MUD software*

When players first connect to a MUD, they choose a name, a gender and a role by which the other players will know them. Like Chat, these identities may not reflect the user's true personality or gender.

MUD names tend to consist of single words, whereas the player's 'role' enables users to describe in some detail what 'persona' they wish to play in the virtual reality environment. Players can only be known by what they have chosen to project whilst engaging in the MUD and it is virtually impossible for other players to discover the true identity of another player.

Commands

Most communication on MUDs uses commands. These commands can be either typed in or, in MOOs that use dedicated MOO software or Web interfaces, can be clicked on using your mouse. Go to CMCMoo (see Resources – MUDs/MOOs below) and try out their very simple tutorial via their Web software *enCore Xpress*. The tutorial lets you try out commands without the embarrassment of other users observing you.

A common command is the 'say' command. An example of the say command is shown below.

Suppose that a player named Darwin typed in the command:

say Can anyone hear me?

Then Darwin would see on his computer screen:

You say, 'Can anyone hear me?'

and every other player in the same room would see:

Darwin says, 'Can anyone hear me?'

Like e-mail and chat, methods have grown out of practice that enable participants to express emotion.

Darwin types in:

emote smiles.

then every player in the same room sees:

Darwin smiles.

Preparing pupils for MUD and MOO sessions

Before attempting to engage a class in any session, ensure that you first become completely comfortable with basic MOO commands for moving and communicating, and with the software your pupils will be using to access a MOO or MUD session. Visit your intended MOO/MUD environment and explore it thoroughly, particularly with a view to finding out what features are available.

Make sure that the MOO/MUD allows access to its facilities to classes of pupils and that its environment is appropriate to your class's age group and interests. Then find out if you need to schedule large class meetings in advance.

If you can enter the MOO/MUD, proceed to investigate the netiquette (rules of behaviour) of the MOO/MUD you plan to work on. The environment might be one where pupils are expected to collaborate in specific rooms only, or it could be one where users can meet anywhere. The individuals that run the MOO/MUD session, known as wizards, might be willing to help pupils by answering any pleas for help, or they might prefer that pupils find themselves in an emergency situation. Check all this out beforehand.

The next step is to teach your class all the basic commands for communication and movement as well as introduce them to the various locations in the MOO/MUD that they might want to visit. You could do this by producing help sheets listing the basic commands and naming the rooms available on the MOO/MUD.

As with all software, give your pupils ample time to practise and become accustomed to the environment before expecting them to carry out any particular assignment. Provide them with numerous chances to practise MOO/MUD activities with one another before allowing them access to other users outside the group. As with all educational activities, if you plan ahead, you're less likely to come unstuck.

Resources – MUDs/MOOs

MUD software (Windows):
http://www.mudconnect.com/

MUD software (Macintosh):
http://www.hsoi.net/mud/clients/

Rapscallion (Macintosh commercial software):
http://www.rapscallion.co.uk/

Diversity University: The first MOO aimed at educators. Has a useful online tutorial. You will need dedicated MOO software to access this site. Direct your software to the following *host* location by typing in the details below:

Host: moo.du.org
Port: 8888

CMCMoo – a MOO dedicated to Shakespeare's *A Midsummer Night's Dream* and that enables you to connect to the MOO using more user-friendly Web-based software called *enCore Xpress*. You will need to use more recent versions of browsers that can handle Java, a programming language.

Try logging in as a guest (password: guest) and trying out some of the commands:
http://cmc.uib.no:**8000**/

ATHEMOO – a MOO site for exploring theatre online. It also uses enCore Xpress as its interface:
http://moo.hawaii.edu:**7000**/

LINGUAMoo – a site for exploring language use. Uses enCore Xpress:
http://lingua.utdallas.edu:**7000**/

enCore Xpress software:
http://lingua.utdallas.edu/

A list of Educational MOOs is available at:
http://cinemaspace.berkeley.edu/~rachel/moolist/edu.html

Making it happen – list of technical resources

There's only one way to find, install and use the tools mentioned in this part of the book. You have to go on to the Internet and just do it. Some basic Internet tools are available on CD ROMs sold with Internet magazines found in your local newsagent. They really can provide a cost-effective alternative to scouring the Net for tools.

Resources – technical

The Internet itself is a great source of software and technical information. Some software is free, some is shareware (you pay a nominal fee) and some commercial. Below is listed all the technical resources mentioned in this book in *alphabetical* order.

Browsers

Netscape (Windows and Macintosh):
http://home.netscape.com/comprod/upgrades/index.html

Internet Explorer (Windows and Macintosh):
http://www.microsoft.com/downloads/

ArcWeb (Acorn) (does not support tables):
http://www.beebware.com/software/riscos.html

Webster XL (Acorn) (supports frames, tables, flash):
http://www.rcomp.co.uk/

Bulletin boards

Sample bulletin boards:
http://www.bulletinboards.com/bulletin-board.cfm

Free bulletin board software:
http://www.intrasmart.com/bulletinboardsoftware-hotb.htm
http://www.thedirectory.org/diamond/usoft.htm

Compression and decompression

PKZip (Windows):
http://www.interpages.co.uk/pkzipage/

WinZip (Windows):
http://www.winzip.com/

Stuffit Expander (Windows and Macintosh):
http://www.aladdinsys.com/

!Sparkplug and !SparkFS (Acorn):
http://www.netlink.co.uk/users/pilling/

Conferencing software

NetMeeting (Windows):
http://www.microsoft.com/windows/netmeeting/download/nm301x86.asp

WebBoard (Windows and Macintosh):
http://webboard.oreilly.com/

First Class (Macintosh and Windows):
http://www.softarc.com/

E-mail

Eudora for Macintosh:
ftp.eudora.com

Pegasus (Windows):
http://www.pegasus.usa.com/

Microsoft Outlook Express (Windows):
http://www.microsoft.com/

TTFN (The Thread Following Newsreader) (Acorn):
http://www.arcade.demon.co.uk/ttfn.html

Extranets

Complete Intranet Resource's guide to Extranets:
http://www.intrack.com/intranet/extra.shtml

The Intranet/Extranet Research Centre:
http://www.cio.com/forums/intranet/

FTP

Collection of FTP software (Macintosh):
http://www.macorchard.com/ftp.html

Collection of FTP software (Windows):
http://cws.internet.com/ftp.html

FTPc (Acorn):
http://www.ftpc.iconbar.com/

Graphics

GIF Converter and image packages (Macintosh):
http://sunsite.org.uk/packages/mac/Collections/sumex/_Graphic_&_Sound_Tool/_Graphic/

Graphics Converter (Macintosh):
http://sunsite.org.uk/packages/mac/Collections/sumex/_Graphic_&_Sound_Tool/_Graphic/

Lview Pro and other image packages (Windows):
http://sunsite.org.uk/packages/ibmpc/collections/simtel/win95/graphics/

Graphics Viewers (Acorn):
http://sunsite.org.uk/packages/archimedes/collections/uni-stuttgart/riscos/graphics/tools/

Paint Shop Pro (Windows):
http://www.jasc.com/

Adobe Photoshop (Windows and Macintosh):
http://www.adobe.com/

Groupware

Groupware Central:
http://www.terry.uga.edu/groupware/groupware.html

Usability First site:
http://www.usabilityfirst.com/intro/newcomers.html

Lotus:
http://www.lotus.com/home.nsf/welcome/notesua

Web4:
http://www.jdhtech.com/

Internet Relay Chat

mIRC (Windows):
http://www.mirc.co.uk/

M_ircle (Macintosh):
http://www.ircle.com/

IRC (Acorn):
http://www.acornusers.org/cbsa/Internet.html

Freezone for Kids (all school age groups):
http://chat.freezone.com/

Kids Chat (for young children):
http://www.sutton.lincs.sch.uk/kidstest/start.htm

Anexa (create your own chat areas):
http://www.anexa.com/

EduCentre (American site for chats on educational issues):
http://home.talkcity.com/LibraryDr/edupeople/

Intranets

The Complete Intranet Resource:
http://www.intrack.com/intranet/index.shtml

The Intranet/Extranet Research Centre:
http://www.cio.com/forums/intranet/

Mailing/e-mail lists

Comprehensive lists of e-mail discussion groups:
http://www.liszt.com
http://www.jiscmail.ac.uk
http://catalog.com/vivian/interest-group-search.html

National Grid for Learning's Virtual Teacher Centre discussion groups:
http://vtc.ngfl.gov.uk

JISCmail discussion lists:
http://www.jiscmail.ac.uk

uk-schools
http://www.jiscmail.ac.uk/lists/uk-schools.html
A list for teachers and others interested in the use of the Internet in UK schools and for general discussion about anything concerning international classroom connections.

basic-skills
http://www.jiscmail.ac.uk/lists/basic-skills.html
This list is intended to provide a forum for discussions relating to the provision and delivery of Basic Skills services, particularly relating to the introduction and use of online and other ICT resources.

ict
http://www.jiscmail.ac.uk/lists/ict.html
A list for announcements and discussion related to the use of information and communication technologies (ICT) and/or information and learning technologies (ILT) in teaching and learning.

ict-support
http://www.jiscmail.ac.uk/lists/ict-support.html
A list to provide peer and expert ICT support for student teachers.

school-management
http://www.jiscmail.ac.uk/lists/school-management.html
A list for discussion of education in schools, in particular their management and government and the curriculum.

teacher-education
http://www.jiscmail.ac.uk/lists/teacher-education.html
Discussion of all aspects of professional education and development for teachers in initial teacher training.

Instant messaging software

ICQ:
http://www.mirabilis.com/

Infoseek Instant Messaging:
http://www.peoplelink.com/v1/down_infoseek/

MSN Messenger Service:
http://messenger.msn.com/

Metadata and indexing

The Basics of Meta Tags:
http://www.virtualpromote.com/metatag2.html

Metadata Introduction and Discussion Group:
http://ferl.becta.org.uk/features/metadata/metadatamain.htm

Dublin Core Metadata Initiative:
http://purl.oclc.org/dc/

The University for Industry Standards on Learning Content Interworking:
http://www.ufiltd.co.uk/materials/qualified.htm

MUDs/MOOs

MUD software (Windows):
http://www.mudconnect.com/

MUD software (Macintosh):
http://www.hsoi.net/mud/clients/

Rapscallion (Macintosh commercial software):
http://www.rapscallion.co.uk/

Diversity University: The first MOO aimed at educators. Has a useful online tutorial. You will need dedicated MOO software to access this site. Direct your software to the following *host* location by typing in the details below:

Host: moo.du.org
Port: 8888

CMCMoo – a MOO dedicated to Shakespeare's *A Midsummer Night's Dream* and that enables you to connect to the MOO using more user-friendly Web-based software called *enCore Xpress*. You will need to use more recent versions of browsers that can handle Java.
    Try logging in as a guest (password: guest) and trying out some of the commands.
http://cmc.uib.no:8000/

ATHEMOO – a MOO site for exploring theatre online. It also uses enCore Xpress as its interface:
http://moo.hawaii.edu:7000/

LINGUAMoo – a site for exploring language use. Uses enCore Xpress:
http://lingua.utdallas.edu:7000/

enCore Xpress software:
http://lingua.utdallas.edu/

A list of Educational MOOs is available at:
http://cinemaspace.berkeley.edu/~rachel/moolist/edu.html

Personalized pages

Ask Jeeves:
http://www.askjeeves.com/

Excite:
http://www.excite.com/search/

My Yahoo:
http://my.yahoo.com

A FAQ (Frequently Asked Questions) file about security and cookies:
http://www.w3.org/Security/Faq/wwwsf7.html

Cookies Central:
http://www.cookiecentral.com/

Plug-ins

Tucows – for a selection of plug-ins:
http://tucows.rmplc.co.uk/

Adobe Reader:
http://www.adobe.com/

List of plug-ins for Netscape:
http://www.phoenixat.com/scott/plugins.html
http://www.disney.com

QuickTime:
http://www.quicktime.apple.com

Real Player:
http://www.real.co.uk
http://www.real.com

Shockwave and Flash:
http://www.macromedia.com

Resources – intranets

The Complete Intranet Resource:
http://www.intrack.com/intranet/index.shtml

The Intranet/Extranet Research Centre:
http://www.cio.com/forums/intranet/

Resources – extranets

Complete Intranet Resource's guide to Extranets:
http://www.intrack.com/intranet/extra.shtml

The Intranet/Extranet Research Centre:
http://www.cio.com/forums/intranet/

Search sites

Argus Clearinghouse:
http://www.clearinghouse.net/

References on searching

Barlow, Linda (February 1997) The Spider's Apprentice – Tips on Searching the Web
http://www.monash.com/spidap.html

Evaluation of Selected Internet Search Tools (January 1997)
http://www.library.nwu.edu/resources/internet/search/evaluate.html

Notess, Greg R (February 1997): 'Comparing Net Directories', Database 20.1 61–64
http://www.onlineinc.com/database/FebDB97/nets2.html

Sullivan, Danny (January 1997) A Webmaster's Guide to Search Engines and Directories
http://calafia.com/webmasters/

Tillman, Hope N (February 1997) Evaluating Quality on the Net
http://www.tiac.net/users/hope/findqual.html

LibrarySpot's Search Engine Tips
http://www.libraryspot.com/features/searchenginetips.htm?news

Meta search sites

Aesir
http://www.aesir.com/aesir/staff/JimSearch.html

All 4 One
http://all4one.com/

Dogpile
http://www.dogpile.com/

Find-It
http://www.itools.com/find-it/find-it.html

Google
http://www.google.com

Meta Crawler
http://www.metacrawler.com/

Search.com
http://www.search.com

Search tools

Alta Vista
http://altavista.digital.com/

Ask Jeeves
http://www.askjeeves.com

EuroFerret
http://www.webtop.com/search/topferret?PAGE=search&LOOK=euroferret

Excite
http://www.excite.com/

G.O.D
http://www.god.co.uk/

HotBot
http://www.hotbot.com/

Infoseek
http://www.infoseek.com/

Lycos
http://www.lycos.com/

OpenText
http://search.opentext.com/

REX
http://rex.skyline.net/

WebCrawler
http://webcrawler.com/

Specialized search sites

Achoo – healthcare
http://www.achoo.com/

Aqueous – water related
http://www.aqueous.com/

Ask Jeeves for Kids – a search facility for children
http://www.ajkids.com/

BigBook – US businesses
http://www.bigbook.com/

Cinemachine – movie reviews
http://www.cinemachine.com

Deja News
http://www.deja.com/

Shareware – software
http://www.shareware.com/

Yahooligans – a search site for children
http://www.yahooligans.com/

Subject directories

Yahoo
http://www.yahoo.com/

Galaxy
http://galaxy.tradewave.com/

Internet Public Library
http://www.ipl.org/ref/

World Wide Web Virtual Library
http://vlib.org

Magellan
http://www.mckinley.com/

The Otis Index
http://www.otis.net/index.html

Search.com
http://www.search.com/

UK search sites

Alta Vista UK – generic tool
http://uk.altavista.com/

Ask Jeeves UK – generic tool
http://www.ask.co.uk/

Excite UK
http://uk.excite.com/

Lycos UK
http://www-uk.lycos.com/

Yahoo UK – generic tool
http://www.yahoo.co.uk

Yellow Pages UK – organizational searches
http://www.yell.co.uk/

ADAM – architecture, design and media
http://www.adam.ac.uk/

EEVL – Edinburgh Engineering Virtual Library
http://eevl.ac.uk/

OMNI – Medical
http://omni.ac.uk/

SOSIG – Social Sciences
http://sosig.esrc.bris.ac.uk/

Sound

QuickTime (Windows and Macintosh):
http://www.quicktime.apple.com

Real Player (Windows and Macintosh):
http://www.real.co.uk/

MP3 software (Windows and Macintosh):
http://software.mp3.com/software/

Sound players (Windows):
http://www.supernet.net/cwsapps/

WHAM (Windows):
http://www.supernet.net/cwsapps/ssound.html

AMP Radio (Macintosh):
http://www.subband.com/ampr/download.html

Sound players (Acorn):
http://www.acornusers.org/cbsa/Audio.html

UseNet

List of newsreaders (Windows):
http://cws.internet.com/news.html

NewsWatcher (Macintosh):
http://sunsite.doc.ic.ac.uk/packages/info-mac/comm/_Internet/

Messenger Pro newsreader (Acorn):
http://www.rcomp.co.uk/

List of public newsgroups in the UK:
http://www.usenet.org.uk/newsgroups.html

List of global newsgroups:
http://www.liszt.com/news/

Video

QuickTime (Windows and Macintosh):
http://www.quicktime.apple.com

Empire (Acorn):
http://www.uniqueway.co.uk/software/empire.html

General Acorn Software:
http://www.riscos.com/

Video conferencing

CUseeMe (Windows and Macintosh):
http://www.cuseeme.com/

Dwyco video conferencing (Windows):
http://www.dwyco.com/

Internet video conferencing in schools:
http://gsh.lightspan.com/cu/index.asp

Virtual classroom

http://www.digitalbrain.com/document.server/admin/member.htm
http://www.jisc.ac.uk/jtap/htm/jtap-044.html

NOF Training for Teachers:
http://www.nof.org.uk/edu/edu.htm

Web-based e-mail

Hotmail:
http://www.hotmail.com

Postmaster:
http://www.postmaster.co.uk/

Talk21:
http://www.talk21.com/

e-groups:
http://www.egroups.com/

everyone.net:
http://www.everyone.net/main/html/email_tour.html

Working offline

Teleport (Windows):
http://www.tenmax.com

WebWhacker (Macintosh and Windows):
http://www.bluesquirrel.com/whacker

SiteSeer (Acorn):
http://www.arsvcs.demon.co.uk/r-comp/index.html

WebTool (Acorn):
http://www.argonet.co.uk/products.html

Part 2

Curriculum Activities

5

Curriculum activities

Introduction

In this section of the book, the focus is on using the Internet in the curriculum. It is organized into the following curriculum areas: Mathematics, English, Science (Physics, Chemistry, Biology), Citizenship, Geography, History, Design and Technology, Modern Foreign Languages, Music, Religious Education, and Art and Design. Each of these areas of study is presented with an introduction and a number of related activities.

The activities consist of preparation and activity notes designed to help you plan and carry out the lesson. Most of the curriculum areas have activities presented at Key Stages 3 and 4. All Key Stage 3 activities are linked to the DfEE (Department for Education and Employment) Schemes of Work.

This second edition uses, where possible, established Web resources which are expected to stand the test of time! However, the Web is a constantly changing environment with new valuable resources being added all the time and this can sometimes cause changes in the Web page address (see Chapter 1 – Browsing the Web) of an existing resource. Remember that it is unlikely that the address would have changed very dramatically and therefore learning to use the techniques, like those described in Chapter 1, to deal with apparently unobtainable pages should make finding resources easier.

The activities try to use the full potential of the Internet. They are challenging and aim to help pupils become critical and largely autonomous users of IT (information technology). Most of the activities involve pupils in accessing the Web and using appropriate search tools. The emphasis in Key Stage 3 is on the use of directories rather than search engines.

Some activities require pupils to have Web page authoring skills. Since this does not require knowledge of computer programming (see Chapter 2, Web authoring), these activities are readily accessible for pupils at Key Stage 3.

In some activities pupils are asked to download files from the Internet. In many cases this is straightforward but it does require knowledge on how to store files on your computer's hard disk (Chapter 1, Downloading files from the Internet). Since a number of the activities make use of the multimedia facilities of the Web, a computer with a sound card is an essential requirement.

The communication ability of the Internet is utilized in some of the activities. Pupils are invited to send e-mails and participate in online conferencing using e-groups. IT/ICT (information and communications technology) can successfully support a collaborative learning model (Chapter 4, Collaborative learning) and therefore support a socially constructivist learning model. A collaborative approach is adopted in several of the activities by suggesting the use of group roles or of electronic communication technologies.

There is no time allotted to the activities. The majority of them can be adapted to fit within a double class period, or spread, in project fashion, over a longer length of time. Some activities do require some form of preparation by the pupils and where this is necessary, it has been highlighted.

It is hoped that you will not just read the activities associated with your curriculum area. The Internet provides support for a number of different and valuable teaching approaches. We have tried to incorporate what we think is appropriate in your curriculum area but some of the other subject areas might provide ideas for further fruitful development. So please browse other activities.

Mathematics – an introduction

There are a large number of mathematics sites on the Web that can support classroom work in a variety of ways. A substantial number of sites contain interactive activities. There are sites which support the teacher by providing worksheets and planning documents, sites that provide background reading for both the teacher and the pupil and finally sites that provide online help in a variety of guises.

The BBC is probably the best provider of interactive activities. Its Maths File is at:

http://www.bbc.co.uk/education/mathsfile/

supports KS3 mathematics in an original and entertaining manner and can readily be used as extension work or as an introduction to a topic. Each activity has four levels of difficulty so differentiation is not a problem.

For teacher support material, the first site to visit must be the Virtual Teacher Centre site at:

http://vtc.ngfl.gov.uk/resource/cits/maths/integrating.html

This site is the home of CITS (Curriculum IT Support for mathematics) and should be a bookmarked (Chapter 1, Browsing the Web) site for any mathematics teacher. The BBC Web Guide is found at:

http://www.bbc.co.uk/Webguide

This is a route to several hundred reviewed mathematics sites and a place where you are very likely to find that particular resource for which you've been looking. Remember the search facilities on the site. These can save you a lot of time and searching a site like the BBC will probably lead you to resources such as The Mathematics site of Richard Phillips:

http://www.edu.bham.ac.uk//maths/links/

This site will provide you with important first-hand support material as well as links to other useful places.

For the teacher of mathematics, the Web provides many opportunities for the development of IT capability within a mathematical context. The IT strands that are particularly relevant to mathematics and the Web are:

- handling information, which involves storing, retrieving and presenting factual information;
- modelling, which can be used to study mathematical functions, eg through testing hypotheses;
- communicating information, which involves modifying and presenting information in a variety of ways incorporating words, pictures, numbers and sound.

The activities below try to show how the Web can be used to develop mathematical skills linked to the IT capability. They cover most of the areas of the mathematics programmes of study and can be considered examples of how to use the Web in those areas. The use of the Web in mathematics teaching is limited only by the limits of imagination of the curriculum planner.

ACTIVITY MATHS I   KS 4 SAVING AND BORROWING

Mathematics NC links	Ma2 Number and algebra Calculations: 3j, k

Outcomes
The pupils will:
Develop ideas on compound interest.
Have the opportunity to use the Web as an information source.

Preparation

The Internet is now a major source of information about interest rates. Gone are the days when interest rates were on outdated leaflets from financial institutions. All of the major banks and building societies have sites on the Internet where you can find information on interest rates for borrowing and selling.

   The pupils are given an example and are then asked to work out the best gross rate for an investment and a loan over the same period. Many banks and building societies have loan and savings calculation areas on their Web sites where pupils can calculate the cost and interest of loans and saving. For the Abbey National go to:

http://www.abbeynational.co.uk/organiser/calculator/savings/

Figure 5.1   *The Abbey National Calculator*

After calculating the sums of money, pupils are asked to investigate the sites of other banks and building societies to find if they offer different rates for investment and borrowing. One particularly helpful site is the Halifax:

http://www.halifax.co.uk/default.asp?PageId=1422

To find the list of banks and building societies which have sites on the Internet, it is more fruitful to use a directory rather than a straight search (Chapter 3, Seek and ye shall find). Ask the pupils to use the Yahoo search site at:

http://www. yahoo.co.uk

If they type in the keyword 'banks' and then search in the UK only, they will arrive at a category 'United Kingdom Business: Companies: Financial services: Banking: Banks'. This link will then take them to a list of banks. Alternatively, you could point them to some of the specialist search devices which are also listed in Chapter 3, Seek and ye shall find.

The activity

If you save money in a savings account with a bank or a building society, it will earn interest because those financial organizations will be using that money. Similarly, if you borrow money from a bank or building society you will have to pay interest. The amount of interest depends upon the amount you have borrowed or saved, the length of time that you leave the money in the bank or borrow it for, and the interest rate.

Example of an interest calculation:

A friend places £100 in the ABC Building Society and they pay interest at 4% per annum (each year). If the interest earned stays in the account, how much will your friend have in the account at the end of the fourth year?

Year | Amount saved
1 | £100 × 1.04
2 | £100 × 1.04 × 1.04 = £100 × $(1.04)^2$
3 |
4 | £100 × $(1.04)^4$ =

At this point pupils can be directed to an interest-calculating site to check on their investment strategy. Direct them to the savings/investment page. Note that the interest they will use will be the gross interest rate.

You can now get them to compare this with the cost of borrowing £2,000 for four years. Which banks and building societies are the most competitive for lending and borrowing? Show them how to use Yahoo and directory structures (Chapter 3, Seek and ye shall find).

ACTIVITY MATHS 2   KS 3 SPECIAL TRIANGLES

Mathematics NC links	KS 3 Shape, Space and Measures Using and applying: 1a, b, c, j Geometrical reasoning: 2b, c, d

Outcomes
The pupils will:
Arrive at a definition of similar triangles.
Use an important Web mathematics site.

Preparation

This lesson uses a famous mathematics site at:

The Maths Forum
http://forum.swarthmore.edu

This American site is a Mathematics Education Community Centre on the Internet. It is a major source of mathematical ideas and also the home of Dr.Maths, a service that answers pupils' mathematical questions.

The site that we will use for similar triangles is Sarah Shapiro's site:

http://forum.swarthmore.edu/~sarah/shapiro/sum.angles.html

This contains a worksheet that can either be printed or used online. On the worksheet there are three circles with triangles within them. Ask the pupils to find five triangles in the top diagram that have the same shape but are different in size.

The pupils can copy the triangles onto graph paper and turn them so that they all have the same orientation. Using the screen print triangles, ask the pupils to determine the interior angles of the chosen triangles and label the angles on their copies.

The pupils can then do the same with the other two diagrams, finding the similar triangles inside them. They will find that there are not so many in this case and can decide for themselves what is special about similar triangles.

Similar triangles are quite important in the art of origami, so after the definition of similar triangles is arrived at, it could be worthwhile looking at some origami patterns and see what role it does play. A site that might be informative is the UK National Origami Society at British Origami Society:

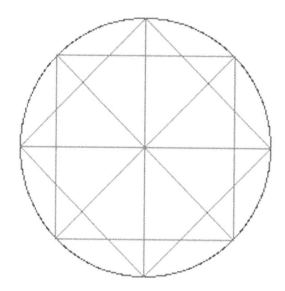

Figure 5.2 *An example of five triangles*

http://www.britishorigami.org.uk/

Links from the resources section of this page will lead to a selection of designs ranging from bangers to boats.

There are a vast number of mathematical opportunities on the Swarthmore site (http://forum.swarthmore.edu) that could lead to alternative Web-linked teaching opportunities.

The activity

Pupils can read about similar triangles on the BBC BITESIZE Revision site:

http://www.bbc.co.uk/education/gcsebitesize/maths/shape_and_space_i_h/similar_shapes_r ev.shtml#triangles

This is a very long URL so encourage pupils to go to the BITESIZE maths site (http://www.bbc.co.uk/education/gcsebitesize/maths/) and type 'similar triangles' into the search facility. Pupils can then go to the Swarthmore site and download and print the angles page.

1. Ask how many triangles can be found in the top diagram.

2. Ask them to find five triangles that have the same shape but are different in size.
3. Ask the pupils to identify, measure and label the interior angles of the chosen triangles from the printed image.

Repeat this exercise for the second and third diagram. How many can they find and how many are the same shape? What is special about the triangles that they have found?

Finish by explaining that similar triangles are very important in the art of origami (paper folding) and direct them to the British Origami Society site.

⌨ ACTIVITY MATHS 3   KS 3 GRAPH IT

Mathematics NC links	Ma4 Handling data
	Using and Applying Mathematics: 1a
	Algebra: 2d, 3b
Outcome	
The pupils will:	
Develop graph skills using real situations.	
Access and use up-to-date data from the Web.	

Preparation

There are two excellent BBC sites that tackle graphs at Key Stage 3 level. The 'Maths File' site has a clever interactive activity that would be an excellent part of any introductory session. You can find this at BBC Maths File:

http://www.bbc.co.uk/education/mathsfile/shockwave/games/datapick.html

For additional reading, send the pupils, in their lunch hour, to BBC BITESIZE revision site at:

http://www.bbc.co.uk/education/ks3bitesize/maths/home_menus/menu_handling_data.shtml

To generate a graph, two sets of data are needed. If both of the variables are discrete, then a block graph is the appropriate way to plot the data. A good block graph can be obtained from the National Lottery numbers generated each week.

One Web site that will give you the latest National Lottery numbers and the numbers since the lottery began is Mersey World – The Lottery:

http://lottery.merseyworld.com/Winning_index.html

The pupils can collect data from the last 20 lotteries and draw a pictogram of the results. This can then be compared with a pictogram of the results from all the lotteries given on The Mersey World analysis page:

http://lottery.merseyworld.com/Analysis/

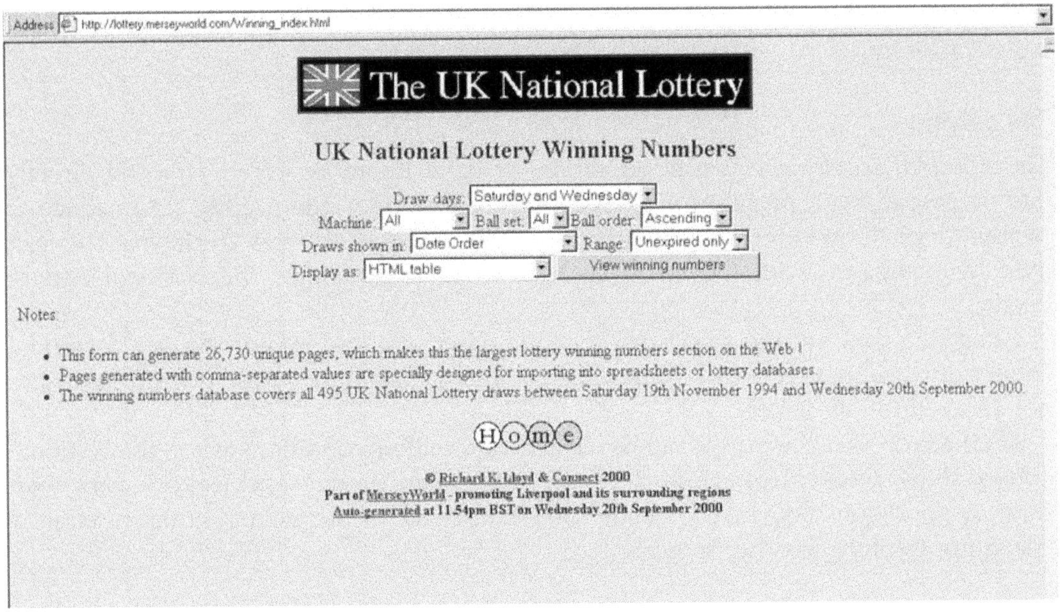

Figure 5.3 *The Mersey World National Lottery Statistics*

Alternatively, the pupils could look at the weather forecast over the past five days and plot temperature and other weather statistics. This data will generate a line graph that could then be used for prediction. The weather forecast data can be found at the The Electronic Telegraph:

http://www.telegraph.co.uk

Or you might find that there is a more local source of weather data. The Birmingham Grid for Learning has its own weather station where collected data can be cut and pasted into spreadsheets and analysed. You can find The Birmingham Weather Station at:

http://www.bgfl.org/ secondary/ks3/subjects/frameset.cfm?subject=Geography

If you are seeking other sources of data for similar activities as those described here, then visit The Data and Storage Library:

http://lib.stat.cmu.edu/DASL/

This is a data storage area where data is stored as 'stories'. You can click on a 'story' to get data from an array of sources. Unfortunately, most of the data is collected from areas in Northern America, but you could add your own 'story' to the site, thus giving it a UK flavour.

The activity

The National Lottery site is a good source of data. It can be cut and pasted directly into a spreadsheet program like Microsoft Excel. Get the pupils to produce a pictogram of the winning National Lottery numbers over the last 20 draws. This can then be compared with the one that shows the trends since the National Lottery began.

Using this data get the pupils to generate a set of numbers for the next National Lottery draw. It may be worth reminding the pupils that if they are under 16, they are not allowed to buy tickets.

Alternatively, get the pupils to investigate the weather conditions when the National Lottery draw takes place. How does the total prize money and jackpot vary with weather conditions? Maybe they could predict the size of the jackpot at the next draw based upon future weather forecasts.

🖳 ACTIVITY MATHS 4   KS 3 FIBONACCI NUMBERS

Mathematics NC Links	Ma1 Number and Algebra
	Using and Applying: 1f, h
	Sequences, functions and graphs: 6c
Outcomes	
The pupils will:	
Examine a number series.	
Search the Internet and create a Web presentation.	

Preparation

Fibonacci was born in Pisa, Italy, in about 1180. He was also known as Leonardo of Pisa. His writings became influential in introducing the Indo-Arabic numeral system and making it more easily understood by scholars. His work in algebra, geometry and theoretical mathematics was far ahead of his European contemporaries.

The third part of his book 'Liber abaci' (The book of the calculator) gave examples of recreational mathematical problems of the type still enjoyed today. As part of this, there was a series of numbers that have become known as the Fibonacci series. This series was found to have many significant and interesting properties.

There are many Web sites that discuss Fibonacci, but a highly recommended one is The Fibonacci Numbers and Nature:

http://www.ee.surrey.ac.uk/Personal/R.Knott/Fibonacci/fibnat.html

On this site there is plenty of background information on Fibonacci and its application. The activity suggested below examines Fibonacci's work by looking at the petals on flowers. The pupils will use a search tool such as Infoseek or Alta Vista (Chapter 3, Seek and ye shall find) to search for flower pictures or sites that contain photographs of flowers (seed catalogues).

The pupils are asked to collect suitable photographs for a presentation on Fibonacci. Pupils will therefore have to be familiar with saving pictures from the Web. The findings are to be presented in Web page format, so it might be necessary to prepare a template using a suitable Web authoring package (Chapter 2, Web authoring).

The activity

Introduce the pupils to the Fibonacci series and suggest that they might like to visit the Fibonacci Web site suggested above. The pupils are asked to make a presentation on Fibonacci numbers and flower petals in the form of a Web document. They are to collect text and pictures from the Web and save them to either a floppy or hard disk.

The activity question is 'Is it possible to find a flower that does not have a Fibonacci number of petals?'

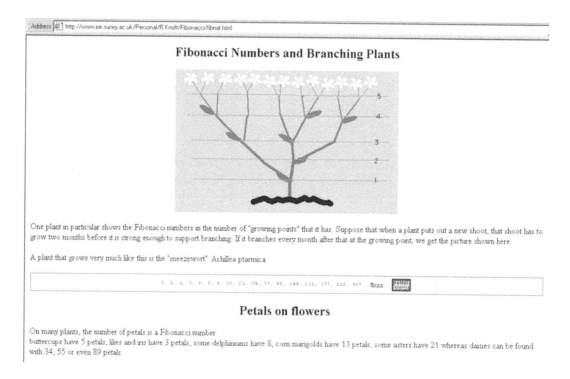

Figure 5.4   *Fibonacci numbers*

Ensure that the pupils are clear about selecting the appropriate background and the font size of the text. Are they aware that for pages to display quickly, they must try to avoid too many pictures on one page? Are they also aware of copyright restrictions? For more information on these issues, you can go to Chapter 2, Copyright or visit the DfEE Safety Site, Safety on the Superhighway:

http://safety.ngfl.gov.uk

English – an introduction

The Web can provide access to numerous sites of interest to the English teacher and the number of sites continues to grow. These sites either relate specifically to English study or can be looked at as examples of the use of language.

E-mail facilities that have become available through access to the Internet are another valuable resource as they considerably widen the communication possibilities. The National Grid for Learning, via the Virtual Teacher Centre, has published its own thoughts on IT and English at The Virtual Teacher Centre:

http://vtc.ngfl.gov.uk/resource/cits/english/ictandenglish/index.html

It states that IT in English can help pupils to:

● talk, read and write for a range of purposes;
● organize and present information in a variety of forms;
● broaden the range of audiences for their work;
● identify key characteristics and features of text;
● develop understanding of language.

An important site for any English teacher is one that gives pathways to other valuable resources. The Virtual Teacher Centre has a special area devoted to English links at English Links at the Virtual Teacher Centre:

http://vtc.ngfl.gov.uk/resource/cits/english/resources/reviews.html

This lists links to sites for English teachers interested in IT, sites for writers, early English sites, classic literature sites and other language study sites.

One question to consider is: how can English and the use of the Web link with IT capability? Word processing and desktop publishing software are probably the most common form of IT used in the classroom. All pupils are now expected to present a document produced with a word-processing package.

In English, it is the process of reading, researching, structuring, drafting and editing the word-processed document that is of importance. These processes can be enhanced by the integration of the Web. The Web gives access to more up-to-date research material in graphic and text form than any other medium and it also provides a non-paper medium for presenting work in a hypertext format.

The activities below are examples of how the Web could be integrated in its various forms into parts of the English curriculum. There are activities that use the Web for information gathering, communication and presenting work at different levels of English and IT capability. The activities have no set time allocation and can be used in a variety of ways.

The interactive whiteboard is proving to be the new aid to innovative teaching and learning in English. The whiteboard (Chapter 3, The virtual classroom) can be used to record pupils' responses and compare them to other class responses.

It can also be used to deliver Web-based activity to the whole class, thus promoting class/class interaction through video conferencing (Chapter 4, Talk! Talk! Talk! and discussion group activities (Chapter 4, Talk! Talk! Talk!). It provides an interface that allows the integration of a whiteboard with the power and facilities of the computer.

ACTIVITY ENGLISH I   KS 3/4 PRODUCING A PLAY

English NC links   En1 Speaking and listening: 1, 3, 10, 11
                             En2 Reading: 4, 5, 6

Outcomes
The pupils will:
Participate in a drama activity and investigate the process of play production.
Use the Web as an information-based text source.

Preparation

In this exercise pupils are encouraged to work in collaborative groups. They are to imagine that they are part of a production team that is bidding to produce a play. Each group will be asked to present plans for the production of one scene of a Shakespeare play in an attempt to gain the contract to produce the new play. In the plans, consideration must be given to the important elements of the production such as set, costumes, soundtrack, actors and actresses, special effects and budget.

Pupils must become intimate with the text and allow their imagination to create the best possible production, within budget and time restraints. The scene that will be used is the balcony scene from *Romeo and Juliet*. This is available on the Web in several places. Try The University of Victoria English Department:

http://www.engl.uvic.ca/faculty/MBHomePage/ISShakespeare/Rom/Rom2.2.html

or The University of Sydney, Australia:

http://www.gh.cs.usyd.edu.au/~matty/Shakespeare/texts/tragedies/romeoandjuliet_2.html#x
ref010

There is also the BBC BITESIZE revision site on *Romeo and Juliet* at BBC BITESIZE:

http://www.bbc.co.uk/education/ks3bitesize/english/home_menu/menu_shake_char_mot.
shtml

There are obvious advantages in having all the text from these sites in electronic form as notes so that annotations and other changes can be made easily. In preparation for the activity it might be useful to download these sites onto the local server using special software that can download all or part of a site (Chapter 3, Other useful tools).

As part of the research for the project, the pupils can search for set construction and lighting plans for plays on the Web. This will need some careful keyword searching using one of the search tools (Chapter 3, Seek and ye shall find).There are special search engines that can be used for searching for theatrical information.

Bruce Spielbauer's page below has some useful notes associated with the text:

http://www.shakespeare.com/qandr/others/4.2.97/

The pupils can be allowed artistic licence with the scene. They might get some useful ideas from accessing the Web pages that look at the film of *Romeo and Juliet*. The production groups can deliver the proposals orally.

The activity

Set the pupils up as production teams bidding to produce a play. The company who is financing the play has asked all the bidders to produce plans for a scene from Romeo and Juliet and they will use this plan as the basis for selecting the successful bidder. The task is to plan the production of the balcony scene from Shakespeare's *Romeo and Juliet.*

Ask pupils to consider the set location, actresses and actors, music, costumes, prompts etc. An important consideration will be some estimate of the cost of the different elements of the production process as the successful group will probably be one of the most cost-effective in this limited budget production.

ACTIVITY ENGLISH 2   KS 3/4 MASCULINE OR FEMININE

English NC links	En I Speaking and listening: 5
	Reading: 3, 5

Outcomes
The pupils will:
Develop an understanding of grammar.
Be able to use the Web to find information.

Preparation

Investigate the Web sites for this investigation to check that they work. Print a copy of Elizabeth Bishop's poem. Be aware of copyright restrictions on its use (Chapter 2, Copyright). If the pupils feel that they need support with the grammar involved in this exercise, they can be pointed to many of the online grammar support areas, some of which are listed in *Activity English 3*.

The activity

Ask the pupils to make a list of nouns, verbs, adjectives and adverbs which have a distinct masculine or feminine meaning linked to them. For some background reading on this go to the Purdue Online Writing Lab's Non-Sexist language page at:

http://owl.english.purdue.edu/workshops/pp/

The pupils are then asked to examine the poem *Filling Station* by Elizabeth Bishop at:

http://www.poets.org/poems/poems.cfm?prmID=978

Bishop makes many references to 'femininity' and defines 'masculinity' without being obvious or condemnatory. Ask the pupils to determine who is the 'somebody' that takes care of the flowers and '... loves us all'. The pupils should then be invited to examine a national online electronic newspaper like the Daily Telegraph at:

http://www.telegraph.co.uk

and see how sexist language is used in the articles. Ask the pupils to report back on what they have found out and write a short paragraph on the findings.

ACTIVITY ENGLISH 3   KS 3 CHASE THE SEMICOLON

English NC links   Speaking and listening: 5
Outcomes
The pupils will:
Develop grammar and sentence construction.
Interact with the Web and communicate using the Internet.

Preparation

Grammar and sentence constructions are important elements of English at Key Stage 3. To support grammar work there are some very good sites where examples and definitions can be accessed. One such site by Anthony Hughes is particularly good and this can be found at On-Line English Grammar:

http://www.go-ed.com/english/grammar/

There are also several sites in America and Canada where the spelling can be a little different but the grammar is the same. One of the best is at University of Calgary English Department:

http://www.ucalgary.ca/UofC/eduWeb/grammar/

Each of the areas of grammar has an interactive quiz that allows pupils to test their understanding. Within this activity pupils are asked to go to an English Conferencing Centre where they can create a personal profile about themselves and enter a forum as users and contribute to a conference. The English Forums can be found at:

http://forums.educhat.com:8080/~grammar

The personal profile should contain information on the pupils' e-mail address and a log-on name that is different from their own. This will give them an insight into the use of the Web as a communication medium.

Conference pages are important ways of communicating on the Internet and this is one of many. For more forums go to the Citizenship activities below where you will find opportunities to contribute to several types of discussion group.

Discussion and chat areas are sometimes unavailable since most Internet service providers (ISPs) filter them out (Chapter 4, Talk! Talk! Talk!), so check that you can access them. If you find that you don't have Chat facilities, you may have to arrange for a particular Chat site to be exempted from the filtering arrangement.

Finally, more information on grammar and punctuation can be found on the BBC site at BBC Web Guide:

http://www.bbc.co.uk/Webguide/

Here, you can type in 'grammar' or 'punctuation' to find a set of recommended sites.

The activity

Start the lesson using the interactive quiz on punctuation at:

http://www.brownlee.org/durk/grammar/punc1.html

Discuss with the pupils their score and any problems they might have had. If the pupils were interested in this activity you could direct them to The Birmingham Grid for Learning:

http://www.bgfl.org/bgfl/secondary/ks3/subjects/frameset.cfm?subject=English

At this site they can choose any curriculum area and create their own punctuation quiz. Focus on one aspect of the grammar, the semicolon. Why do we have a semicolon?

At this point they can join the discussion group, look at the frequently asked questions and add their question to the group. The pupils can also look at what other questions were being asked?

ACTIVITY ENGLISH 4   KS 4 MEDIA STUDIES

English NC links   Reading: 5
                                 Writing: 1, 2
Outcomes
The pupils will:
Analyse and evaluate two films.
Create and write a Web page based upon the analysis.

Preparation

Most films have a great variety of materials about them published on the Web. Choose two films that you know are available and have a reasonable collection of resources. Pupils can use a site on *Citizen Kane* at The Citizen Kane Page:

http://www.inform.umd.edu/EdRes/Colleges/ARHU/Depts/CompLit/cmltfac/mlifton/rosebud/Essays/citizenkanepage.html

This has a small black and white clip of the wedding scene. To view this resource you will have to ensure that your computer has the required QuickTime plug-in (Chapter 3, Other useful tools) installed on it. Pupils will also have the opportunity of truly practising their search skills (Chapter 3, Seek and ye shall find) as *Citizen Kane* resulted in approximately 800,000 page hits. To support the pupils you can download examples of analysis and evaluation at the English Teaching in the United Kingdom Web site:

http://www.english1.org.uk/index.htm

These are downloaded as zip files so your computer will need the correct decompression software installed (Chapter 3, Squeezing it all in).

Web page production is no more difficult than word processing. Microsoft Word documents can be converted to Web pages by clicking on 'Save As' and choosing to save as an html file. Pupils can be supported in this work by creating a template within which they can present their work. This can be in the form of a text area and a picture area thus encouraging the use of other resources.

The activity

The pupils are to analyse and evaluate two films in terms of:

- symbolism and imagery – how what we see stands for other things;
- reference – to other works of cinema or of literature;
- narrative methods – eg viewpoint, direct or indirect narration;
- structure – eg order of scenes, time shifts, editing;
- cinematography – composition of shots, tracking, viewpoint, colour/mono-chrome, lighting;
- screenplays and dialogue;
- incidental or theme music – how this reinforces or manipulates our response;
- special effects and artistic design – makeup, prosthetics, animatronics, set and costume design;
- effect on audience.

Encourage the use of the Web as a resource and remind them of advanced search procedures. After searching, discussion, and drafting of responses including selection of images, a final presentations can be prepared and loaded as Web pages on the local intranet (Chapter 3, Other useful tools).

Science – an introduction

The strands of the UK IT National Curriculum that are particularly relevant to Science and the Web are:

- communicating information that involves modifying and presenting information in a variety of ways incorporating words, pictures, numbers and sound;
- handling information that involves storing, retrieving and presenting factual information;
- modelling, which involves using simulations of real or imaginary events to identify changes and trends.

The use of the Internet and particularly the Web in Science has opened up new opportunities for the science educator to link the requirements of IT capability with the science curriculum. The Internet will not replace the investigation and cannot as yet replace traditional data-logging and modelling software. However, it is possible to envision a future where this might be possible.

The Bradford Robotic Telescope at:

http://www.telescope.org/

allows teachers and pupils to control the telescope from a distance. There are sites in the United States where it is possible to observe online dissections and get involved with some very interesting examples of scientific models. For an entertaining example of scientific modelling (mostly for 'A' level pupils), visit The Science Modelling site at:

http://www.Colorado.EDU/physics/2000/applets/index.html

or The BBC Key Stage 3 and GCSE BITESIZE pages at:

http://www.bbc.co.uk/education

This site contains a variety of small animated models which use Flash (Chapter 3, Other useful tools and Chapter 2, Web authoring). They are all ideal for supporting the teaching of the subject as well as revision. No longer do you have to try to explain the complexities of the electric motor using a static whiteboard diagram.

It is hoped that the activities that are described in the following pages can contribute to development in this area. Some of them use the Web as an information source, but in other activities pupils are encouraged to submit information to a National Database and then to use this database for theory constructing and testing. The activities try to involve as much Sc1 (Science Investigations) as possible. They are challenging with respect to both IT and science skills.

ACTIVITY SCIENCE 1 KS 3 THE CIRCULATORY AND RESPIRATORY SYSTEM

Science NC links	Life Processes and Living Things: 2i–l Scheme of Work: Science Unit 8B (Year 8) Respiration

Outcomes
The pupils will:
Know the role of the heart as part of the circulatory system of our bodies.
Use the Web as a multimedia information source.

Preparation

The Franklin Institute at:

http://www.fi.edu/biosci/

has a very good site that is devoted to the Human Heart and the body's circulatory system. The pupils should spend time on these pages reinforcing their knowledge of the three main parts of the circulatory system.

They will then be able to go to 'Blood Vessels' and explore the way in which these work. There is a video on travelling through arteries, which may be found during this exploration. The video is in .MOV format so an appropriate player will need to be downloaded (Chapter 1, Downloading files from the Internet). It may also be important that you download this file before the lesson as the time taken on a 56 K modem is quite considerable.

After examining the functioning of the heart the pupils can pretend they are listening to heartbeats through a stethoscope at:

http://www.fi.edu/biosci/monitor/heartbeat.html

If you cannot play this video you can get the appropriate software from a shareware site called Tucows:

http://tucows.rmplc.co.uk/

This site also houses other necessary plug-ins (Chapter 1, Downloading files from the Internet).

The pupils can check their own health factors by measuring their pulse rate. This is explained on one of the activity pages of the site and includes a short video sequence that shows the pulse points on the body.

The pupils' thoughts and writings could then be added to Body Quest site at:

http://library.thinkquest.org/10348/home.html

After researching the respiratory system they compare their thoughts to those on the Body Quest site and can then add their original contribution to the site.

The activity

The lesson could focus around a number of aspects of the QCA (Qualification and Curriculum Authority) Scheme of Work. This example looks at the question of 'How does the oxygen needed for respiration reach the tissues of the body?' The Franklin Institute at:

http://www.fi.edu/biosci/

provides a good opportunity for a fresh look at the circulatory system with this question in mind.

In collaborative groups, set the pupils the task of finding the answer to the question using the Web. When they report back they can again use the Web to find the contributions of one of the following to the development of our knowledge on the circulation and respiratory system:

How did these people contribute to the development of our knowledge on circulation?

Galen, Vesalius, Harvey, Withering, Ibn-al-Nafis

Encourage the pupils to use the Encyclopedia Britannica at:

http://www.britannica.com

This will lead to other research sites. Each group is then required to write a 250-word report on their findings which can then be submitted to the Body Quest site (Chapter 4, So how do you do it?).

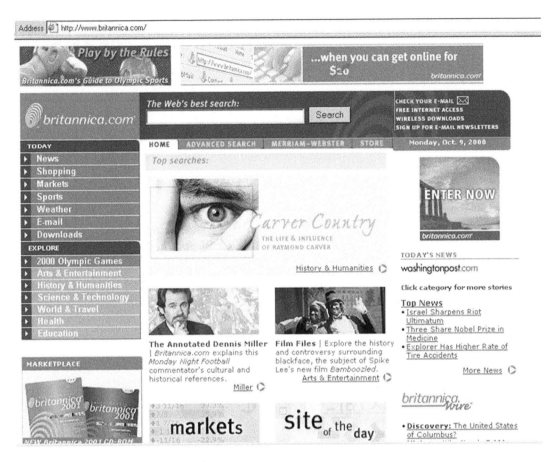

Figure 5.5 *The Encyclopedia Britannica*

**ACTIVITY SCIENCE 2   KS 3 FOXES AND RABBITS –
FOOD CHAINS, WEBS AND
PYRAMIDS**

Science NC links	Key Stage 3
	Life Processes and Living Things: 5a–f
	Experimental and Investigative Science: 3a, b, d and f

Outcomes
The pupils will:
Know how to interpret patterns in data linked to food pyramids.
Be able to download files to the hard or floppy disk.

Preparation

This activity examines a system of three Trophic levels by investigating the relationship between grass, rabbits and foxes. Pupils will need an understanding of food pyramids and the struggle to balance appropriate biomass with the herbivores and carnivores.

Pupils need to download a program from the Web and to store it in an appropriate place on the hard disk of the computer or the network. They will be downloading a trial version of the program from the Future Skill Software site:

http://www.fssc.demon.co.uk/

Click on 'Educational Software' and then 'Creatures'.

Procedures for doing this are outlined in Chapter 1, Downloading files from the Internet. The program will need to be run from the File Manager (Win 3.1) or Explorer (Win 95).

As it is a special edition it will only run for 120 seconds but this should be enough for a feel of the food pyramid relationship in this environment. To rerun, it needs reloading by clicking on the *Creature.exe* icon. The whole process can be made easier in Windows 95 by creating a shortcut and placing the *Creatures* icon on the opening screen.

With knowledge of the basics of a food pyramid the pupils should soon be able to handle the number of foxes, rabbits and amount of grass to create a successfully sustainable environment.

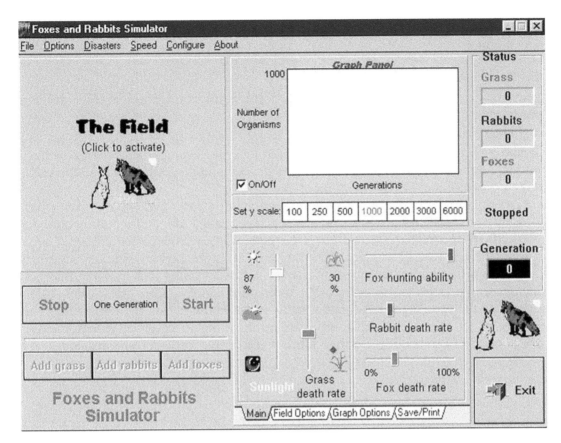

Figure 5.6 *Creatures software*

The action takes place in a 'Field'. This is the area at the top left-hand side of the screen. Show 'The Field' by clicking on it. Once the field appears, you will add grass, rabbits and foxes by clicking on the appropriate button and then clicking again on 'The Field'.

It would be worth buying a copy of the program so that pupils could use it in a more sophisticated way at a later stage. The program is available from Future Skill Software, Penrodyn, Pontrhydygroes, Ystrad Meurig, Ceredigion SY25 6DP.

Pupils can obtain some preliminary support material from The Science Education Associations Server at:

http://www.geog.ouc.bc.ca/physgeog/contents/4e.html

where they can get access to a glossary of terms associated with food chains. They can also participate in an interactive online quiz and test their score by going to the

Quia site (a site that promotes quizzes and interactive tests that you can save on the site) found at:

http://www.quia.com/jq/10183.html

The activity

Focus initially on the population of plants and animals in the school habitat and discuss how they would change over a given time; for example, crows and starlings visiting dustbins in daylight, squirrels visiting after school finishes, foxes after dark; slugs, cats, mice and bats active at night.

Ask pupils to find out as much as they can about a food pyramid that starts with sunlight and ends with foxes. How many consumers do they think would be involved? What conditions would affect the pyramid they have constructed?

Show them how to download a file from the Web, store it on a computer, activate it and create a shortcut as described in Chapter 1, Downloading files from the Internet. Encourage the pupils to download the 'Creatures' activity. They are to use this to investigate the conditions that create a stable ecosystem in which the populations can co-exist. To do this it might be appropriate for them to collect information at the end of a number of generations and then place this data into an Excel spreadsheet.

ACTIVITY SCIENCE 3   KS 4 THE PERIODIC TABLE

Science NC links	Experimental and Investigative Science: 3a, c, d
	Materials and their Properties: 1d, 3a, b, c

Outcomes
The pupils will:
Be able to generate ideas on relationship patterns using an interactive periodic table.
Use the Web as an interactive information source.

Preparation

The periodic table is represented in many forms on the Internet but probably the best is to be found at The University of Sheffield Web Elements Scholar Edition:

http://www.Webelements.com/Webelements/scholar/index.html

'Web Elements' is the first and most comprehensive interactive periodic table on the Web. Using this resource, pupils can get a wealth of information about the elements and their reactions. It has a small audio element where a distant voice names the elements and it contains some of the following information that your pupils might be able to use.

General information:

- Key data and description
- Historical
- Uses

Chemical data
Compounds:

- Electronegativities
- Bond Enthalpies
- Lattice energies
- Radii
- Reduction potentials

Crystallography:

- Crystal structure

Physical data:

- Bulk properties
- Thermal properties
- Thermodynamic properties

Isotopes:

- Naturally occurring isotopes
- Radioactive isotopes

The data on this site is useful for 'A' level as well as for Key Stage 4 pupils.

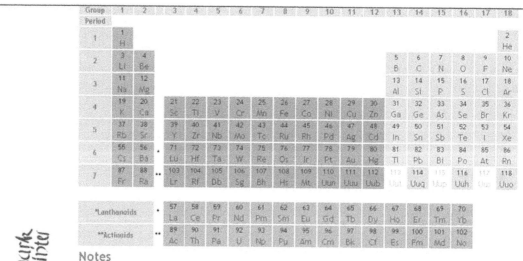

Notes

The WebElements *scholar edition* aims to be a high quality source of information on the WWW about the periodic table for students. You will find many pictures showing element structures and periodic properties. Note that elements 113, 115, and 117 are not known, but are included in the table to show their expected positions. Elements 114, 116, and 118 have only been reported recently.

Figure 5.7 *The Interactive Scholar Periodic Table*

The activity sheet asks the pupils to use the periodic table to look for patterns and trends and create some graphs. Your use of it will depend upon the time available. The activity sheet also refers pupils to a world map at the Xerox.Parc.Map Viewer site:

http://pubWeb.parc.xerox.com/map

Xerox PARC Map Viewer: world 0.00N 0.00E (1.0X)

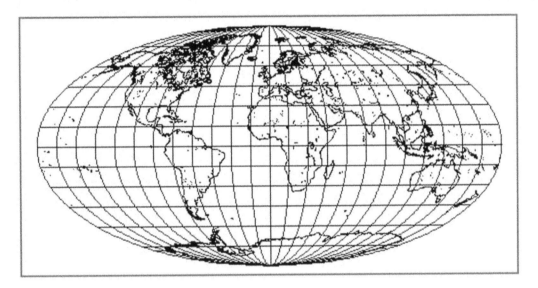

Figure 5.8 *The Xerox Parc Map Viewer*

The pupils will need to copy the map from the screen and print it at an appropriate size. Another excellent interactive periodic table comes from the Physics 2000 site at:

http://www.colorado.edu/physics/2000/applets/a2.html

The activity

Discuss with the pupils the nature of the elements in the periodic table. There are about 45 common elements and almost 55 uncommon ones. It was found that groups of these elements had certain characteristics in common. For example, some were gases which had great stability and were reluctant to react with any other element. Others were metals and were highly reactive.

The organization of the elements into groups resulted in the periodic table. Using the Interactive Periodic Table look at the elements: aluminium, argon, arsenic, barium, bromine, calcium, carbon, chromium, cobalt, fluorine, gold, helium, hydrogen, iodine, iron, krypton, lead, lithium, magnesium, mercury, neon, nickel, nitrogen, oxygen, phosphorous, platinum, potassium, silicon, silver sodium, strontium, sulphur, tin, tungsten, xenon, zinc. Then:

- Plot on a world map the location of the discovery site of each element. Use the Xerox Map Viewer.
- Make a timeline to show the discovery date of each element.
- Trace the language history of the names of five of the elements.
- Write a biographical report on the discoverer of the most common element in the human body.
- Make a bar graph showing the value (£/gram) of each element.
- Identify the two elements MOST active and the two elements LEAST active. Compare and contrast their properties.
- Identify the two elements that are used most often in industrial situations.
- Identify the two elements most useful in the medical field.
- Identify the element that would have the most economic impact if the natural reserves were consumed.

ACTIVITY SCIENCE 4   KS 3 THE STORY OF A PLANET

Science NC links   Sc4 Physical Processes: 3a–e
Outcomes
The pupils will:
Collate data about the planets.
Use the Web as a publication medium.

Preparation

This activity uses the vast resources of the Web, which are focused on the Earth and Space. Prominent among these sites is the NASA site, The Jet Propulsion Laboratory:

http://www.jpl.nasa.gov/

This is a remarkable site with links to most of the space exploration projects. If you want the latest information on ongoing exploration, go to the Press release section on the opening page. Another excellent site is the Nine Planets site at:

http://seds.lpl.arizona.edu/nineplanets/nineplanets/nineplanets.html

This site will give you all the statistical data that you will need for the completion of this activity. The activity asks the pupils to create a multimedia Web page for one planet using information they can get from Web pages or from other sources.

The advantage of Web sources is that pictures can easily be saved to disk and then cut and pasted into their document. The CD ROM Encarta by Microsoft and other sources can also be used, but pupils should be encouraged to visit the NASA pages and get photographs of planets and moons that have only recently been surveyed by different probes.

You will need to prepare the basic Web page template using a Web authoring package such as Microsoft Word or FrontPage or an equivalent authoring tool (Chapter 2, Web authoring) and have available a graphics package such as Paint Shop Pro.

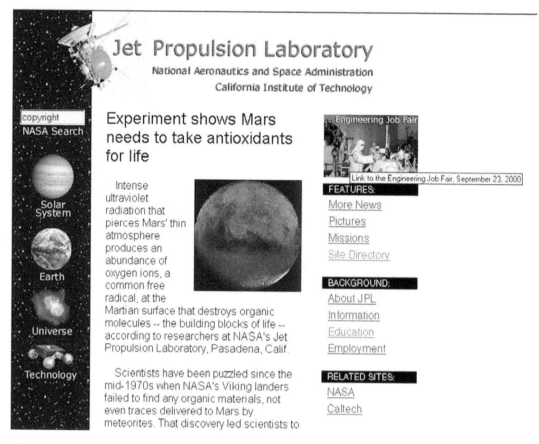

Figure 5.9 *The NASA Jet Propulsion site*

The activity

Divide the class into small groups. Inform the groups that they will be producing a presentation on a planet of our Solar System and allocate one planet to each group. The presentation will be in the format of a Web document that will contain at least 10 linked pages.

Assign individuals to particular tasks within the group. Some of the roles that might be adopted are:

- *Director* – responsible for making sure that all those involved in the production are working towards the same objective.
- *Researcher* – responsible for finding out information about the planet.
- *Story writer* – responsible for constructing the storyboard, requesting information and overseeing production.
- *Producer* – responsible for producing the story on the screen.

Tell the pupils that before they start collecting information, they will need to decide upon the story. To do this they will need to have some information on the planet of choice, either by using a CD ROM, the Web or both. They can then decide upon the story. It could be something like 'A day in my life'.

Citizenship – an introduction

Citizenship is a newcomer to the National Curriculum although not a newcomer to the school curriculum where it has always been taught under a variety of different guises. The Web has always provided a home for a lot of citizenship resources and it could be argued that the Web itself is a living, growing example of active citizenship.

The UK Parliament at The Parliament site:

http://www.parliament.uk/

is an obvious starting site to look at some aspects of citizenship. On this site you will find a vast amount of information about what is going on in Parliament, including the records of the debates on the day after they have occurred.

It is, however, a difficult site to use directly in the classroom because of the amount and complexity of the information. A much better site would be the Explore Parliament site at:

http://explore.parliament.uk

This site has some excellent interactive activities where you can search for the Mace, try an online Parliament quiz or most importantly get involved in an online debate.

If the pupils do not know who their Member of Parliament is then their names can be located at the Members site:

http://www.locata.co.uk/commons/

Once they have found their MP they can e-mail him or her directly from this site. For the younger pupils there is an engaging news site called Westminster Watch at:

http://www.westminsterwatch.co.uk

which gives access to the current news, and which has a political dimension.

There are, however, many other aspects of citizenship for which the Web can be utilized. One large area connected to consumers' rights is found on the Consumer Association site:

http://www.which.net/index.html

where, although most of the site is closed to non-subscribers, there is a valuable free area that gives details of the campaigns with which the association has been involved. The Financial Services Agency at:

http://www.fsa.gov.uk/consumer/

also supplies lots of information on consumers' rights in the area of finance. The site has a good selection of links to other useful sites, including banking, insurance and pensions.

For Key Stage 4 pupils, the citizenship stage widens and pupils are expected to move outside of the UK in their studies. Europe becomes an important stage and the sites that link to the European Parliament are the Europe site at:

http://www.europarl.eu.int/

and the European Union site:

http://www.europa.eu.int/

CITIZENSHIP ACTIVITY I KS 3 ACT OF PARLIAMENT

Citizenship NC Links	I d The key characteristics of parliamentary and other forms of government 2c Contribute to group and exploratory class discussion

Outcomes

The pupils will:

Be aware of the procedures and roles of Parliament.

Have debated in the classroom a debate that mirrors that of Parliament.

Preparation

There are two sections to this activity:

- finding out about the key personnel in Parliament;
- taking part in a debate.

It is likely that this activity will occupy several sessions because Parliamentary debates, by their very nature, can spread themselves over several weeks.

The activity uses two main sites: the Explore Parliament site at:

http://explore.parliament.uk

and the Parliament site at:

http://www.parliament.uk/

On the Explore Parliament site there is an activity called 'Act of Parliament' where pupils can join a current debate and determine the procedures. It may even be possible to view the debate you are involved in live at the BBC:

http://news.bbc.co.uk/hi/english/uk_politics/default.stm

which contains the BBC's political news section.

The first task is to register for the debate. Details on the debate can then be found on the Parliament site. The roles of individuals to be explored are:

- The Lord Chancellor;
- Serjeant at Arms;

Figure 5.10 *Explore Parliament*

- Black Rod;
- Voter;
- Government Back Bench MP;
- Opposition Back Bench MP;
- Cabinet;
- Shadow Cabinet;
- Prime Minister;
- Leader of the Opposition;
- The Speaker;
- Whips;
- Chairmen of Select Committees;
- Law lords;
- Lords Spiritual;
- Lords Temporal;
- The Lord Chancellor;
- The Queen.

Point out the strange spelling of 'Serjeant'. Then visit the 'Explore Parliament' site, which has a database of information that can answer the questions posed in the activity below. At this stage, it might equally be useful to introduce other resources such as the Encyclopedia Britannica site at:

http://www.britannica.com/

The activity

Determine what the pupils know about Parliament and its role. Present them with the list of titles outlined above and, working in groups, ask them to try to assign a role to each of the names. After the feedback session, pupils are directed to research the Web to check on the roles.

At this point you might wish to give them an opportunity of developing their search skills and direct them to one of the general search engines (Chapter 3, Seek and ye shall find). Alternatively, direct them to the Explore Parliament site and the Encyclopedia Britannica.

Introduce the debate and ask about the roles of the different titles in the debate. What role has the Speaker? Does the Serjeant at Arms have a role? Ask about how they are going to find information about the debate and point them towards the newspaper sites (see next activity).

CITIZENSHIP ACTIVITY 2   KS 4   EUROPEAN PARTNERS

Citizenship NC Links	1f Opportunities to bring about social change in Europe 1l Relations between the United Kingdom and Europe and the European Union 2b Expressing and defending an opinion

Outcomes

The pupils will:

Research a current issue of importance relating to the relationship between the United Kingdom and Europe.

Debate with another school in Europe about the issue.

Contribute to the European Union debate on the issue.

Preparation

This activity will require a significant amount of support. Initially, investigate the debates that are proceeding in the European Union by going to the European Union:

http://www.europa.eu.int/

and click on the 'Dialogue in Europe' button. At the time of writing, there were two debates concerned with 'European Integration' and 'The Enlargement of the European Union'. Thoughts on these issues can also be researched using the national newspaper sites. Try the *Guardian* Web site:

http://www.guardian.co.uk/guardian/

which provides 2,291 articles on Europe. A collection of this size presents a challenge to the searcher and may require revision of the keywords used for the search.

Other useful newspapers are *The Telegraph*:

http://www.telegraph.co.uk

The Independent:
http://www.independent.co.uk/www/

The Times:
http://www.thetimes.co.uk/

All of these papers have a search facility that allows access to archived material. You will need to find a suitable European school for a linked discussion.

For ease you could try Ireland, but it may be more fruitful if you tried a mainland Europe school. You can use the database of online European schools at My Europe site:

http://www.en.eun.org/myeurope/myeurope-schools/index.html

called 'My Europe Schools' which has been established just for this purpose. You can either register your school or contact schools already listed there.

If you have any problems with translation when trying to conduct a discussion with pupils from Europe, then introduce your class to the Bablefish site:

http://bablefish.altavista.com/translate.dyn

This site contains an online translator. E-mail seems the most obvious tool to use, although in this instance the establishment of an e-group might be feasible. The use of e-groups is discussed in Chapter 4, Talk! Talk! Talk! and the e-group Web site is found at:

http://www.egroups.co.uk/.

Try to establish the e-group before you start the activity. You will need to have all the pupils' screen names and e-mail addresses at hand for both you and your partner school/s. Another alternative is to use video conferencing. Again, you will find a description of the use and potential of video conferencing in Chapter 4, Talk! Talk! Talk!.

The activity

If you have access to a data projector and an interactive whiteboard (Chapter 3, The virtual classroom), the opening screen of the European debating area would be a good starting point.

Decide upon the question for debate. This will depend upon the size of the class. For a small class, two groups researching the alternative arguments of one question would be a good arrangement. For a larger class, both questions could be debated.

A source of archived arguments would be a useful way of moving forward. Newspaper searching makes a good starting point, as these can present radically different views of the same issue. From here, further research could be made using the European Parliament or UK Parliament pages.

This would be a good point to share your debate question/s with your European partner/s. You may need to make use of the translation tool.

One school can then be given the task of drawing together the pros and cons of the

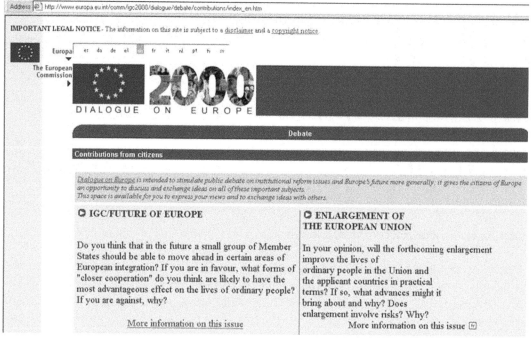

Figure 5.11 *The European debate*

debate. After further exchange, a final version can be submitted to the European debate.

Geography – an introduction

Geography is well represented on the Internet and the Web in particular. Many organizations have details of their economic and development activities published on Web sites. You will also find a large number of local authorities in the United Kingdom offering a wide range of information that can be used in development and economic geography.

The importance of the Web in Geography is well illustrated by the number of references made to Web sites in the QCA Schemes of Work for Geography. Physical geography has a variety of sites dealing with the weather and volcanoes scattered across many different parts of the world. These can be easily found using the search facilities available to you (Chapter 3, Seek and ye shall find).

Pupils studying geography can use the Web to:

● enhance their skills of geographical inquiry and investigation;
● gain access to a wide range of geographical knowledge and information sources.

A useful reference page for the geographer is the geography support page at the Virtual Teachers Centre:

http://vtc.ngfl.gov.uk/vtc/curriculum/geography/index.html

This page provides you with links to other geography resources such as the World Factbook at:

http://www.odci.gov/cia/publications/factbook/index.html

The World Factbook has access to geographical, economic and social information about each country in the world. This is particularly useful for Key Stage 4 work on population studies. The two activities in this section both involve pupils in using the Web and its interactive capability.

ACTIVITY GEOGRAPHY 1   KS 3   FOLLOWING THE VOYAGE

Geography NC links	Geographical enquiry and skills: 1c, 2c, f3
	Scheme of Work: Unit 24 Passport to the world
Outcomes	
The pupils will:	
Develop map reading skills.	
Practise the interactive use of Web pages.	

Preparation

This activity uses an acclaimed Web resource – the Parc.Xerox. Parc.Xerox is an interactive map of the world that enables the geographer to use map references of longitude and latitude values to plot the progress of a variety of voyages, including those by sea, air or land. The Xerox Map Viewer is available at:

http://pubWeb.parc.xerox.com/map

A voyage that could be used is by explorer Tim Severin. Starting in January 1996, Tim and his crew retraced the path of Alfred Russel Wallace who, along with Charles Darwin, first announced the theory of Natural Selection. Their account of the voyage is found at:

http://www.curriculumWeb.org/ercntr/spiceislands/sivoyage/sivhome

Alternatively, pupils could be asked to search the Web for other voyages, such as yacht races or balloon trips. Some yacht races give regular position updates and you might be lucky enough to hit a live online yacht race.

The Whitbread/Volvo yacht race is an annual event and has a Web site at:

http://whitbread.quokka.com/main.html

It is also possible to get archived information on a race that has already been run. For example, the Transpac Honolulu race has the history of the race archived at:

http://krypton.nmr.hawaii.edu/transpac/95/pos_rpts.html

All of these races visit various locations and a study of these can be an extension of this activity. However, pupils will need to be familiar with the Parc Xerox interactive map. There are tutorials available at the map site. The notes below attempt to give the necessary instructions for the successful completion of this activity.

The activity

In this activity the pupils follow the progress of a voyage and try to trace the route that it takes. They will first have to search the Web to find a suitable voyage that provides regular updates on its position and progress. Suggest keywords such as 'yacht races' or 'balloon circumnavigation'.

It would be exciting if a race is in progress but if this is not possible they could visit the Hawaii or Whitbread sites where there are reports that already include the position of the boats. Ask them to plot the voyage on the interactive map. Their success at using the map depends upon an understanding both of longitude and latitude and of the structure of Web pages.

Using the Parc Xerox Interactive Map:

Select an area of the map and, by clicking on it, obtain an enlargement of that area. Look at the top of the map to find the latitude–longitude values for the view that you have selected.

Now look in the URL box of your browser and notice that the figures for longitude and latitude are included in the URL. The values can be changed in the URL and the map will refocus on the longitude and latitude values that you have inserted.

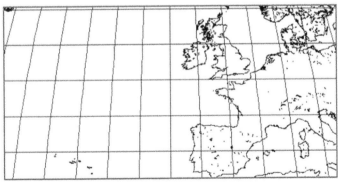

Address 🖉 http://pubweb.parc.xerox.com/map/ht=22.50/lat=48.31/lon=-12.59/wd=45

Xerox PARC Map Viewer: world 48.31N 12.59W (8.0X)

Select a point on the map to zoom in (by 2), or select an option below. Please read about the Map Viewer, FAQ and Details. To find a U.S. location by name, see the Geographic Name Server.

Figure 5.12   *The Parc Xerox Map 1*

The following URL will result in the map reference shown in Figure 5.12:

http://pubWeb.parc.xerox.com/map/ht=22.50/lat=48.31/lon=-12.59/wd=45.00

The latitude and longitude values can be marked by going to the Options section on the Parc Xerox map. Note that you now see a map that corresponds to another URL:

http://pubWeb.parc.xerox.com/map/ht=22.50/lat=48.31/lon=-12.59/mark=38.31,-12.59/wd=45.00

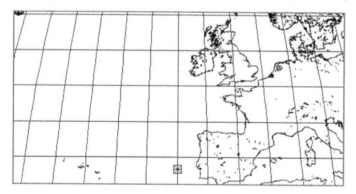

Address [🖉] http://pubweb.parc.xerox.com/map/ht=22.50/lat=48.31/lon=-12.59/mark=38.31,-12.59/wd=45.00

Xerox PARC Map Viewer: world 48.31N 12.59W (8.0X)

Select a point on the map to zoom in (by 2), or select an option below. Please read about the Map Viewer, FAQ and Details. To find a U.S. location by name, see the Georgraphic Name Server.

Figure 5.13   *The Parc Xerox Map II*

The information about the mark can be changed in the same way that the latitude and longitude were changed in the previous example – by using the URL box. This allows the positioning of the mark at the exact position of the voyage. The map can be printed out at any time.

Pupils can then be encouraged to search for interesting geographical data on the places visited by the voyage.

ACTIVITY GEOGRAPHY 2   KS 3   EXPLORING VOLCANOES

Geography NC links	Breadth of study: Themes: 6b and c Scheme of Work: Unit 2 The restless earth – earthquakes and volcanoes
Outcomes The pupils will: Understand ideas on volcanoes and their impact on societies. Use the Web as a source of information.	

Preparation

There is a lot of up-to-date information on the Web on earthquakes and volcanoes. One common approach to studying such phenomena is to use case study material.

This seems an ideal topic to approach through interaction with the Web. The activity can be structured as a group activity where each group is given the role of scientific 'human interest'. Reporters will be required to report on the cause and location of earthquakes and volcanoes in a particular area of the world. Pupils will have to search the Web to obtain information on the communities affected by volcanic activity (Chapter 3, Seek and ye shall find).

The geographical areas of the world that can be allocated to the pupils are Africa, North America, North Asia, Central and South America, Antarctica, Europe and West Asia, South East Asia.

Information on volcanoes and earthquakes can be found at Volcano World, a site that has an online vulcanologist to answer all those unanswerable questions. Volcano World will also provide links to many other areas of interest.

Access to Volcano World is via:

http://volcano.und.edu/

Another useful site is Volcanoes on line at:

http://library.advanced.org/17457/english.html

This forms part of the ThinkQuest site. ThinkQuest is a US educational initiative committed to advancing learning through the use of computer and networking technology. ThinkQuest challenges teachers and students of all ages to use the Internet in innovative and exciting ways as a collaborative, interactive teaching and learning tool.

Figure 5.14 *Volcano World*

The library of ThinkQuest is an excellent source of Web-based teaching resources. Finally, you can find a collection of Web cams that are located at the various volcanoes throughout the world at:

http://vulcan.wr.usgs.gov/Photo/volcano_cams.html

The activity

Allocate pupils to a group. The group will be compiling a report for a national newspaper on volcanic activity and its effects upon the local population in a particular part of the world. As an additional task, they can create an online quiz using the quiz creator on the Birmingham Grid for Learning. The quiz can be downloaded (Chapter 1, Downloading files from the Internet) at:

http://www.bgfl.org/bgfl/secondary/ks3/subjects/frameset.cfm?subject=Geography

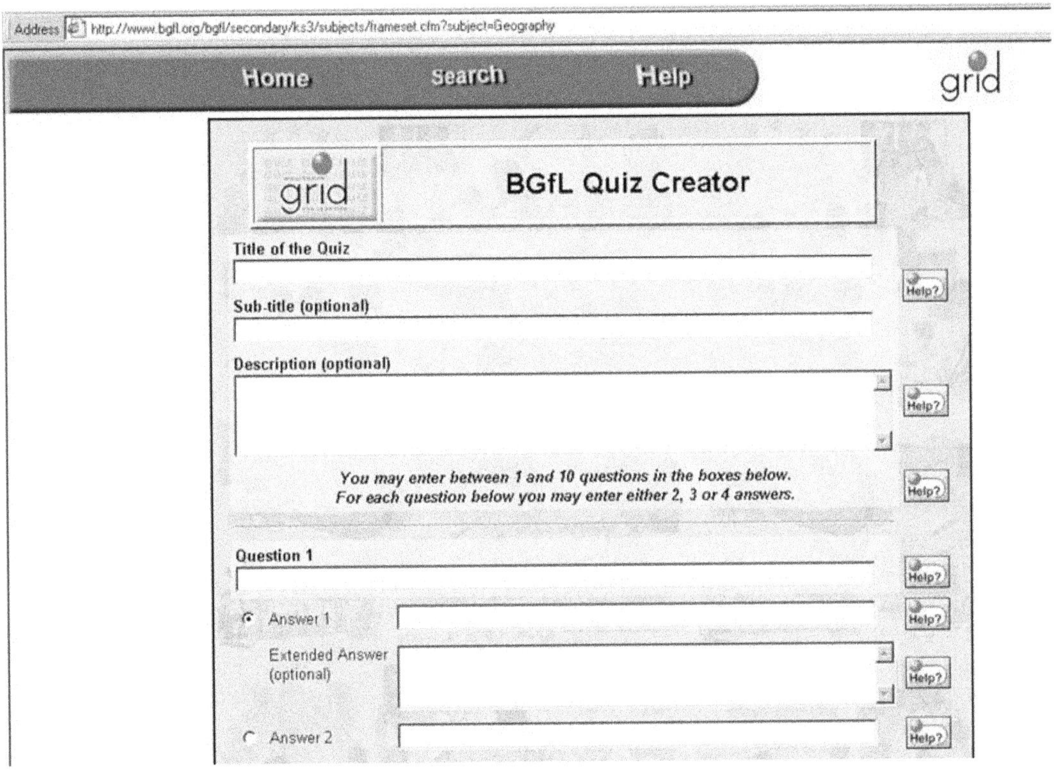

Figure 5.15 *Quiz Creator*

The quiz below is an example. The pupils will either have to find the answers and feed them into the Quiz Creator or they could create a quiz using their own questions. Many of the answers to the questions are available at the Volcano World site.

What is the name for the group of volcanoes that occur around the Pacific Ocean?

1. Circle of Stones
2. Ring of Fire
3. Ocean Edge Volcanoes

The largest volcanoes on Earth (and Mars and Venus too) are:

1. stratovolcanoes
2. cinder cones
3. shield volcanoes

The biggest historic eruption in the United States was at:

1. Mauna Loa
2. Mt St Helens
3. Novarupta

Scientists monitor volcanic activity using:

1. seismometers
2. tea leaves
3. spy satellites

The most common type of volcanic rock is:

1. Andesite
2. Pumice
3. Basalt

Magma is made in the Earth's:

1. crust
2. mantle
3. core

Lava flows that have smooth and ropy surfaces are called:

1. agate
2. blocky
3. pahoehoe

A volcano that has not erupted for many years, but is likely to erupt sometime in the future is called:

1. lazy
2. dormant
3. extinct

Most stratovolcanoes are located above plate tectonic:

1. subduction zones
2. hot spots
3. down ramps

The largest volcano on Earth is:

1. St Helens
2. Dante's Peak
3. Mauna Loa

History – an introduction

There are many sites on the Web for the aspiring historian. These sites provide mainly factual information and the best of these is the Encyclopedia Britannica:

http://britannica.com

A number of Web sites have introduced interactive elements into historical studies. Amongst these is the BBC, with its virtual tours around famous historical sites and its archaeological digs at:

http://www.bbc.co.uk/history/multimedia_zone/3ds/index.shtml

For the historian, the ability to use the search tools of the Web (Chapter 3, Seek and ye shall find) is a necessary skill and an important part of historical inquiry. Pupils should be aware of the different ways in which the search tools can be used and how hard copies of printed sources, pictures and photographs can be obtained from Web pages (Chapter 2, Using graphics).

The importance of the Web as a resource is illustrated by the inclusion of a considerable number of sites as resources in the QCA Schemes of Work. The following activities illustrate the way in which access to the Web can be successfully incorporated into the History curriculum.

ACTIVITY HISTORY 1   KS 3 TIMELINES

History NC links	Knowledge, skills and understanding: 1, 2, 4
Scheme of Work:	History Unit 10 (Year 8) France 1789–94 – Why was there a revolution?

Outcomes
The pupils will:
Develop ideas on timelines.
Investigate the use of the Web in history.

Preparation

There are some useful history sites that give access to information in a way that is appropriate for Key Stage 3 history students. The Hyper History site, which is featured in this activity sheet, is an excellent example of the use of hypertext in documentation. The hypertext links take you to photographs, pictures and maps of people and places of interest. You can find Hyper History at:

http://www.hyperhistory.com/online_n2/History_n2/a.html

The site is built around the concept of a timeline and this gives the framework for this activity. Pupils are asked to select a period in history and compare different interpretations of that period. In this instance it is suggested that the *French Revolution* is used.

They are then asked to go to the Hyper History site and use the timeline to extract relevant information. As the Hyper History site is an American site, the interpretations of events may be different from those provided by a British source. Pupils should therefore be encouraged to check out any details by using the Encyclopedia Britannica site or by referring to a CD ROM such as *History of the World* by Dorling Kindersley. The library is also another source of information.

The task is to reconcile the differences and create a timeline for that event which pupils think is appropriate. The timeline could be presented as a Web document if the appropriate Web authoring software is available.

The activity

Stress that it is important to realize that the interpretations of events are dependent upon the perspectives of the interpreter. This activity asks pupils to select different interpretations of one event from a variety of sources and to analyse the similarities and differences. They then create their own timeline of the event.

To achieve this you need to go to the main page of the Hyper History site and select the 'History' option, then pick the appropriate period for the 'French Revolution' by identifying it on the timeline. This is achieved by moving the mouse arrow to the period required and clicking on it.

You should find yourself viewing information contained in the right-hand box of the screen. Print out this information.

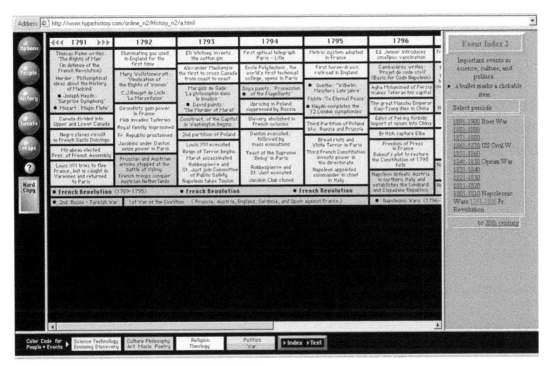

Figure 5.16 *The Hyper History site*

The kind of information you could search for includes:

● the reasons that led to the start of the revolution;
● the start and finish dates of the revolution;
● the geographical area/s where it took place;
● the periods of fighting and the dates of these periods;
● who gained what and who lost what in the revolution.

ACTIVITY HISTORY 2 KS 4 COAL MINES, WOMEN AND CHILDREN IN VICTORIAN TIMES

History NC Links	Knowledge skills and understanding 2, 3, 4 Britain 1750–1900

Outcomes
The pupils will:
Learn how to examine for bias in historical evidence and to practise accessing information on the Web.

Preparation

This activity takes text from parliamentary documents about the conditions in coal mines in the first half of the nineteenth century. Pupils access this information and download it into a word processing file. The pupils can then analyse the information and highlight words and phrases that express feelings or bias about conditions in the mines.

The site they will be using is called The Victorian Web and it contains a wealth of information about Victorian times. The site address is:

http://landow.stg.brown.edu/victorian/victov.html

The Spartacus Internet Encyclopedia Web site at:

http://www.spartacus.schoolnet.co.uk/history.htm

will give other interpretations.

Pupils examine the highlighted text and determine the factual basis for the beliefs and feelings of the witnesses. They then arrange the statements by theme; for example, by the treatment of children, of women or by the hours worked. This could be done within the word processing program. Make sure that the pupils have access to instructions on using search tools before starting this activity (Chapter 3, Seek and ye shall find).

The activity

Ask the pupils to examine the text of evidence submitted in the early nineteenth century on the conditions of labour for women and children. Suggest that they look for evidence of bias in the factual statements of witnesses as found at the Victorian Web site.

Point them towards the evidence on 'child labour' in coal mines which is in the section labelled *Testimony Gathered by Ashley's Mines Commission* and ask them to download the information to a word processing package.

The task is to examine the text and highlight all the parts of the evidence that could express opinions based upon historical fact and support a particular point of view. Repeat the whole exercise for 'women in coal mines', using the same source.

Pupils should then be encouraged to use the search tools to find other supporting material. Finally, they are asked to create a presentation of their findings as a poster of phrases.

Design and Technology – an introduction

The study of Design and Technology looks forward to the future but recognizes that the present is based upon the achievements of the past. Increasingly, designers need to be able to access large amounts of knowledge before developing a design proposal, and manufacturers need to sell their products and ideas in very competitive markets.

The Web is an information base that is fast becoming a record of past designs and a repository of ideas for the future. It offers a unique up-to-date source of statistics, marketing and design ideas and information on raw materials.

Like other areas of the National Curriculum, there are sites that provide information and useful links for technology teachers. In the UK, there is the Virtual Teacher Centre page at:

http://www.vtc.ngfl.gov.uk/resource/cits/dant/integrate/integrate.html

Another useful site is the Design and Technology online site:

http://www.dtonline.org/

and the Design and Technology Association:

http://www.data.org

It is already possible to see examples of how the facilities offered by the Web and the Internet are being used to advantage. For example, schools are linking with local universities and colleges of further education to take advantage of the engineering CAM facilities of Higher and Further Education.

Product designs, produced by school pupils, are downloaded to the CAM equipment at the universities and colleges of further education and the production process observed by pupils via a video link across the Internet.

Or how about basing a Web activity on the *Changing Rooms* programme? Imagine the design principles, research and use of communications technologies that could be promoted within such a project.

The importance of the Web in Design and Technology education is illustrated by the large number of QCA Schemes of Work in Design and Technology which have Web sites listed as resources.

ACTIVITY D&T I   KS 4 PROMOTING A PRODUCT

D & T NC Links   Developing, planning and communicating ideas: 1a–g
Outcomes
The pupils will:
Develop ideas on promoting a product.
Learn how to design and create Web pages.

Preparation

The promotion of an artefact or an idea in commerce and industry is often through some form of presentation to potential financial backers. Such presentations invariably involve technology in some form. It is now likely that a presentation will have a multi-media element and use presentation software such as Microsoft *PowerPoint*. Looking to the future, the influence of the Web will become increasingly important and Web browsers will become a major promotion and publicity medium.

This activity asks pupils to create a multimedia presentation for a variety of audiences using Web pages as the presentation format. The objective is to sell an artefact or idea to the audiences.

The product for this activity will be linked to the Food Technology site:

http://www.foodtech.org.uk/index.html

This Web site has been designed to support the teaching and learning of Key Stage 4, Design & Technology: Food Technology. The focus is on the industrial practices associated with the manufacture of food products, with particular emphasis on the 'systems and control' component of the KS4 course.

With this resource in place the pupils will need access to scanners, digital camera and appropriate graphics software such as *Paint Shop Pro* (Chapter 2, Web authoring). They will also need a Web authoring package. You might like to consider using a program such as Microsoft FrontPage or Adobe PageMill to construct the Web pages. Alternatively, Microsoft Publisher and Word can both be converted to html pages.

Pupils will need to spend some time searching the Web for resources and ideas. This will mean that they should be familiar with the search tools (Chapter 3, Seek and ye shall find). You will find that phrases such as 'Selling through the Internet' will generate sites that could lead to further research. Access to pictures and sounds on the Web, including animated GIFs and page backgrounds, can also be obtained through the use of search tools (Chapter 2, Using graphics).

The activity

Set the scene for the pupils, asking them to promote an artefact or an idea, linked to food technology, on the Web. They should be directed to search the Web for similar ideas and for information on the potential customer base. Using this research information, the pupils are asked to create and construct two multimedia design proposals for Web pages, one each for a different audience of Web users (Chapter 2, Web authoring).

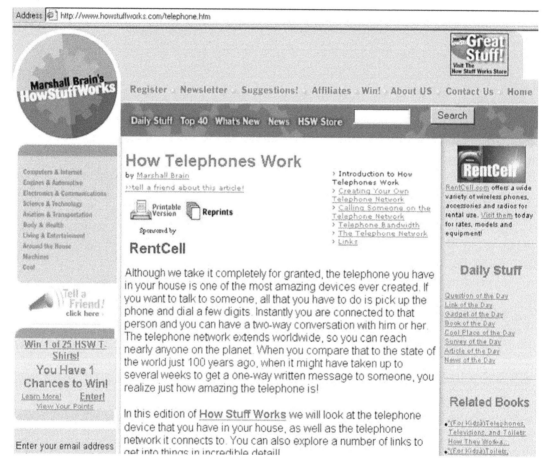

Figure 5.17 *How Stuff Works*

Each Web page will consist of hyperlinks to other pages and it is expected that the presentation will consist of at least 10 pages.

ACTIVITY D&T 2   KS 3 CONTROL

D & T NC links   Knowledge and understanding of systems and control: 5a
Outcomes
The pupils will:
Examine the principles of digital communication.
Use the Web as a teaching resource.

Preparation

For this activity, pupils are required to design an effective and attractive electronic product that could be used to care for someone or something. An example would be a product that controls a pet's environment and keeps the animal comfortable, or one that helps a parent check that a baby's bath water is the right temperature.

To research the activity they will need access to a Web site such as *How Stuff Works*. This is a remarkable resource that attempts to explain how a variety of technological devices and systems work. Look up the site at:

http://www.howstuffworks.com/

Pupils can also find resources at the Design and Technology Online site at:

http://www.dtonline.org/

Both of these resources will provide useful starting points before the pupils embark upon a more general search.

The activity

Pupils are asked to research the background to the proposed device, seeking the opinions of potential users of the product. They are then to draw up a detailed design specification for an electronic product, in a setting of their choice.

They could use the Web sites mentioned in the preparation area as potential research tools. Pupils can then use a Web page to communicate their design to other pupils. E-mail, mailing lists, chat and so forth could be other methods used (Chapter 4, Communicating and learning via the Net).

Modern Foreign Languages – an introduction

A series of broad issues for modern language teachers were identified in a Becta document on Modern Foreign Languages (MFL) found at:

http://www.becta.org.uk/supportproviders/inspection/oth_sub/teach/sec/mfl.html

and a more recent Virtual Teacher Centre document on IT and Modern Foreign Language teaching:

http://www.vtc.ngfl.gov.uk/resource/cits/mfl/inpractice/index.html

These start from the basis that all pupils are entitled to use IT to:

- communicate in the target language;
- communicate with people of the target languages and communities;
- develop and improve all four language skills;
- enhance their language-learning skills, eg to develop their understanding of underlying structures;
- develop or enhance independent learning skills;
- access a range of resources in the target language and identify with the people of target language communities and countries;
- meet their special needs for access to language learning;
- make effective use of and extend existing IT capability.

The VTC site presents six case studies to support these objectives.

The Web is particularly useful because of its worldwide basis. There are sites for most European cities where it is possible to get a wealth of multimedia information in the home language. The sites will provide information on the commercial and cultural aspects of the city and its environs as well as contact names. Contact names will provide the user with another important Internet resource – communication with the target country.

There are several sites that must be visited by the modern foreign language teacher since they provide valuable routes to other important Web resources. The CTI Centre for Modern Languages at Hull University includes a list of specialist search tools for the language teacher to search sites within a target country. Hull CTI is found at:

http://www.hull.ac.uk/cti/

The Internet is fundamentally a communications medium. It is flexible and provides a wide variety of styles of communication which directly support the communicative method of MFL teaching. The activities included here illustrate how the Internet can be incorporated into the modern language curriculum.

Remember, however, that the Web contains sites that are solely in the language being studied. Where else will you be able to learn about contemporary German, French and Spanish houses other than from estate agents' sites in the corresponding countries? What about food and the cost of food? Visit the shops of the country on which you are focusing and find them by searching in the language you are studying using a national search site for that country such as:

http://www.yahoo.fr

ACTIVITY MFL 1   KS 3/4 THE MUSIC WE LIKE

MFL   NC links
Outcomes
The pupils will:
Use the Internet for communication and publishing.

Preparation

Pupils will need access to a Web page template (Chapter 2, Web authoring). They will need to establish communication with a school in the target country. This can be accomplished by using an organization such as European Schools On-line at:

http://www.en.eun.org/eun.org2/eun/en/index.html

Here, you will find European schools that are online and are interested in becoming involved with international projects. First, pupils will have to e-mail a number of schools and ask them if they would like to participate.

The next stage is the construction of a questionnaire in the target language asking about musical tastes. The questionnaire is then e-mailed as an attached document to the target country schools and the results are subsequently incorporated into an article on musical tastes published as Web pages. You could use an online translator such as:

http://world.altavista.com/

Depending upon the information communication capability of the pupils the Web pages could contain audio elements (Chapter 3, Other useful tools).

ACTIVITY MFL 2   KS 3 A MULTILINGUAL WEB

MFL NC links	Communicating information and handling information
Outcomes	
The pupils will:	
Use the Internet for publishing.	

Preparation

This is a group activity. Access to Web page templates using a suitable software package such as Microsoft FrontPage will be required. You will also need a digital camera and scanner.

In this activity pupils are asked to prepare presentation material on their school and locality in one of the modern languages taught in their school.

As a group activity it is suggested that the pupils adopt specific roles within the group. One possible structure is:

- *Director* – responsible for making sure that all those involved in the production are working towards the same objective.
- *Researcher* – responsible for finding out information that will be included on the pages.
- *Story writer* – responsible for constructing the storyboard, requesting information and overseeing production.
- *Translator* – responsible for checking on the translation of the site.
- *Producer* – responsible for producing the story on the screen.

As part of the preparation, pupils should access other European school Web pages and their own locality's Web. The Web site of their locality can usually be found by using CityNet:

http://www.city.net/

This site will lead you to the sites of all the European cities and from these the surrounding locality. When the initial research has been completed pupils can then construct a storyboard for their Web site, collect the pictures and text and insert these into the Web template. The Birmingham Grid for learning (http://www.bgfl.org) high-lights some school sites which have used this formula.

Music – an introduction

Most modern musicians have their own Web pages and a lot of their followers have developed pages that link to their work. Orchestras have performed live on the Internet and musical scores are readily available. More importantly, Web pages are being used for publishing and discussing compositions composed by pupils.

Music has well-established links to electronics and the production of digital music files is now commonplace. It is therefore a small step to link the production of digital sound to Web pages.

To listen to a lot of the music you will find that it is necessary to download the Real Audio Software (Chapter 1, Downloading files from the Internet). This is an ideal piece of software to download because it requires no specialist unzipping at the end of the download.

When it has been successfully copied to your hard disk, it will start itself and run in the background, thus enabling sound files on Web pages to be automatically played. This is available at no cost from Real Audio:

http://www.real.com/

High levels of IT capability can be developed through the use of the Internet in music education. The Internet can particularly contribute to performing, composing, listening and appraising.

Using a keyboard with a midi file player it is possible to create your own music and record it using the facilities available on your computer as most new computers will have a midi frequenting package included in the system. You can find out more about sound players in Chapter 2. The recorded files can then be inserted into your own Web pages.

For listening and appraising, the pupils have access to a world library of musical resources which can be related to a historical and cultural context by further research on the Web using appropriate search tools (Chapter 3, Seek and ye shall find). The comments and music files can be published on a school intranet.

ACTIVITY MUSIC 1   KS 3 EXPLORING INDIAN MUSICAL GENRES

Music NC links	Listening and applying knowledge and understanding
Scheme of Work:	Unit 12 bhajan/qawwali (exploring Indian musical genres)
Outcomes	
The pupils will:	

Identify, explore and perform bhajan/qawwali with understanding of its conventions and context.

Preparation

The Web must play an important part in this area of work as it provides up-to-date access to sites that contain both historical and contemporary examples of both bhajan and qawwali.

As part of the preparation you must be sure that you have downloaded the appropriate Real Audio files onto your computers (Chapter 1, Downloading files from the Internet). The pupils can search the Web and learn about the cultures and contexts in which these genres are performed and begin to appreciate how they are performed. They can then invent melodic material within a rag, add their own accompaniments within a tal, and perform them, record them and upload them back to the Web. To do this you could join the Global Midi Challenge at the Centre for technology in Music Education at CtiME:

http://www.ed.uce.ac.uk/ctime/Old%20Pages/midiglob.htm

💻 ACTIVITY MUSIC 2   KS 3/4 A MUSICAL WEB

Music NC links	Creating and developing musical ideas

Outcomes

The pupils will:

Plan, organize and present a short, effective advertising campaign suitable for a Web site.

Discuss and evaluate conflicting evidence to arrive at a considered viewpoint.

Preparation

Like any other medium, the Web is a commercial environment which sells products and services. Because of download times, the Web has yet to fully use sound to promote its commercial presence. This is, however, changing and many Web sites now have sound linked to them.

In this activity the pupils are asked to choose a product or service and select a Web site that markets that product. Then, they are required to plan and compose the musical accompaniment to the site. Pupils will have to make decisions about the size of the sound file and its format (see Chapter 3). They will also have to explore the nature of the site in relation to musical decisions that may be made about it. Pupils should be prepared to discuss the nature and form of the music in relation to the site's main purpose.

Religious Education – an introduction

It was once said that God was mentioned more times on Web pages than any other noun. When the word was entered into the Alta Vista search engine, it gave approximately four million results (as opposed to two million recorded in 1998).

From the early inception of the Web, the Vatican had an extensive site which has now been joined by Muslim, Hindu, Sikh and other faiths. All of the religions have found a home in the vastness of the Web.

The Religious Education (RE) teacher and pupils have access to up-to-date information on what is happening in the communities of the different faiths. The Internet and the Web also allow pupils to communicate through e-mails and discussion groups with pupils of different faiths all over the world.

An excellent starting point in looking for resources on Anglicanism, Buddhism,

Catholicism, Protestantism, Hinduism, Islam, Judaism, Sikhism and Christianity is the Guardian Unlimited's (the online version of the *Guardian* newspaper) RE resource area at:

http://www.educationunlimited.co.uk/netclass/schools/religion

This site contains a large number of well-researched links to valuable resources. There are three other sites that are worth a visit. The Religious Education Network at:

http://www.cant.ac.uk/renet/

is an excellent site to find information about any of the major faiths. The site was originally constructed for student teachers and there is a short article associated with each of the main faiths and some drawings and photographs. Each faith also has a superb set of links which enable further detailed research.

The RE-XS site at:

http://re-xs.ucsm.ac.uk/

claims to contain virtual tours and worksheets for different faiths. The virtual tours are in fact a few photographs. There are some useful quizzes linked to different faiths and some resources such as schemes of work and worksheets. Finally, visit The RE Site at:

http://www.theresite.org.uk/

ACTIVITY RE 1   KS 3 THE CREATION

RE NC Links	There is no RE National Curriculum so this activity is linked to RE Unit 9B (Year 9) – Where did the universe come from?

Outcomes

The pupils will:

Talk about the scientific theories of the Big Bang and evolution.

Talk about the story in Genesis.

Show understanding of the meaning and significance of the story to religious believers.

Show understanding of the terms theistic evolution and creationism.

Explain questions of meaning and purpose.

Preparation

An excellent starting point for this activity is an animation of the creation at The Creation Story:

http://www.kids4truth.com/creation.htm

You will need the Flash plug-in (Chapter 1, Downloading files from the Internet). The accuracy of the presentation can be checked using the Genesis creation stories. These can be searched for on the Web or this might be an appropriate resource to supply in paper format! You will have to make both versions of the story available.

The pupils will need to find evidence on the Web linked to the Big Bang and evolution as part of the debate. As a part of the preparation, investigate the potential of these two sites: the NASA site at:

http://map.gsfc.nasa.gov/html/big_bang.html

for the Big Bang and the BBC at:

http://www.bbc.co.uk/education/darwin/leghist/bowler.htm

for evolution.

As it would be useful for pupils to make a presentation, it might be helpful to prepare a learning scaffold for them in either the *Microsoft Publisher* or *PowerPoint* presentation programs. Learning scaffolding in this instance is linked to the idea of using software files that have been built up to provide learners with the scaffolding they need to undertake a specific task. From an ICT perspective this means using application templates to support learners.

The activity

Using a large screen display (see Chapter 3), either a large monitor or television, an LCD panel, data projector or an interactive whiteboard (Chapter 3, The virtual classroom), show the **creation** animation. This introduction will lead directly to a consideration of the validity of the animation story compared to the story told in Genesis. The next step will be to remind the pupils of the scientific theory of the Big Bang and evolution.

Divide pupils into small collaborative groups to research Big Bang and evolution theories. Appropriate keywords can be jointly discussed before using conventional search tools. Try searching for 'theistic evolution' and 'naturalistic evolution/evolutionism'. Relevant documents can be printed and suitable items of evidence both for and against the ideas collected. Each group can then use the template to present their findings to the rest of the class.

ACTIVITY RE 2 KS4 AN ISLAMIC MUSICAL PRESENTATION

> Outcomes
> The pupils will:
> Show an understanding of the Islamic faith and the role of music within it.
> Explain questions of meaning and purpose.
> Work together to produce a multimedia Web resource.

Preparation

The Internet allows pupils to collect up-to-date information, in multimedia format, from sites all over the world. Islam is chosen for this activity but any other faith could present similar opportunities.

Pupils will need to be familiar with the search tools (Chapter 3, Seek and ye shall find). There is a lot of information available in this subject area so pupils will need to be capable of using sophisticated search techniques. Typing 'Islam' into a typical search tool resulted in approximately one and a half million results.

An alternative and always useful approach is to go to the BBC site and search the BBC resources (http://www.bbc.co.uk/nomad/Pages/frame02.htm). These resources may then provide a gateway to other useful areas on the Web. The BBC search delivered a large number of results, including a site that described the Musical Nomad OnLine Expedition by Jan Hendrickse. Jan is a flute player who has travelled widely in countries with an Islamic culture and the site provides downloadable music files and a wealth of information on Islamic music. Also try The Islamic Musical Institute:

http://www.islamicinstitute.com/music.htm

Art and Design – an introduction

The Web has become a major depository of artwork. In 1996 an electronic art experience residing on the Internet was auctioned on the Internet for a considerable sum of money. Most of the major art galleries have sites on the Web with examples of work that can be downloaded and there are a considerable number of critiques of works of art published on Web pages.

The Web has also become more interactive as the technology develops, with sites that encourage pupils to paint online.

ACTIVITY ART AND DESIGN I   KS 3 MY WEB SKETCHBOOK

Art and Design NC Links	Exploring and developing ideas Evaluating and developing work Investigating and making

Outcomes
The pupils will:
Identify the purpose of images, speculating on the intentions of the artist.
Identify similarities and differences in the roles and functions of art from different times and places.
Use the Web as a publishing medium.

Preparation

The use of the sketchbook is fundamental to all art activities. This activity encourages pupils to create their own electronic sketchbook to complement the traditional sketchbook. Crucial to this activity is the pupils' skills in searching for, and downloading, graphics items from the Web (Chapter 3, Seek and ye shall find and Chapter 1, Downloading files from the Internet).

As part of this activity students will be expected to experiment with some of this source material and include it within their electronic sketchbook. The pupils will need to search for examples of abstract and expressionist painting. Different groups could be given a different area to research, for example surrealism, fauvism, futurism, pop art.

Ask each group to analyse and comment on the examples. Ask them to identify in each case two or three key features of the work and say what kind of idea, mood or feeling is communicated by the artist and to produce a piece of writing from this.

The source material will need to be found by using the appropriate search tools (Chapter 3, Seek and ye shall find). Pictures on the Web are normally in the JPEG or GIF format (Chapter 2, Using graphics) image files. Images can be edited in a graphics package such as *Paint Shop Pro* for the PC or *Graphics Converter* for the Macintosh.

Discuss with the pupils the copyright implications of their activity. More information is available at the Safety on the Superhighway site of the National Grid for Learning (NGfL) at:

http://safety.ngfl.gov.uk

ACTIVITY ART AND DESIGN 2   KS 3/4 MY NET GALLERY

Art and Design NC links	Exploring and developing ideas 1c Investigating and making art 2b Knowledge and understanding
Outcomes The pupils will: Use the Web as a multimedia design and publishing medium.	

Preparation

In this activity pupils are expected to examine a site which has been established by various artists as a gallery for their work. The site is an exciting one, with examples of work from modern artists in a variety of different formats.

Some of the work involves sound, whilst others involve the moving image. The site is found at:

http://www.art.net/TheGallery/the_gallery.html

After examining the site, pupils are asked to create their own gallery in an electronic format. Initially they are asked to select a theme for their site and a plan for the gallery. This will mainly involve researching the Web.

Once the theme is decided, pupils will need to start producing and collecting images. If it is decided that display material is required from other sources, access to a scanner and digital camera is required. At least 30 per cent of the material should be derived from the Web.

Make sure that the pupils are aware of the importance of the size of the electronic images as large pictures take a long time to load. Images are best prepared in two sizes; as a thumbnail (Chapter 2, Using graphics) and in a size which takes up about a third of a normal-sized screen. Pupils will also need to be aware of how to use the compression facility so that images of the highest quality can be obtained.

The gallery Web pages can be prepared in advance by using a software package such as Microsoft FrontPage or some other suitable Web authoring software (Chapter 2, Web authoring). The finished Web document could be put on the Web or used on the school intranet.

Index

Index

Milton Keynes UK
Ingram Content Group UK Ltd.
UKHW051855071024
449327UK00025B/1974